Maya History

A Captivating Guide to the Maya Civilization, Culture, Mythology, and the Maya Peoples' Impact on Mesoamerican History

Free Bonus from Captivating History (Available for a Limited time)

Hi History Lovers!

Now you have a chance to join our exclusive history list so you can get your first history ebook for free as well as discounts and a potential to get more history books for free! Simply visit the link below to join.

Captivatinghistory.com/ebook

Also, make sure to follow us on:

Twitter: @Captivhistory

Facebook: Captivating History:@captivatinghistory

Contents

Introduction

In the past decade or two, there has been an upsurge of interest about the Maya, their history, civilization, and culture. There have been more documentaries and fiction movies, books and stories about them. This was partly fueled by mythical Maya prediction of the end of the world in 2012, which for a short period of time put this civilization under the media spotlight. But there is much more to their culture than the common misconception about their calendar. And for a long time before the Maya caught the eyes of the wider population, archeologists and historians did their best to uncover and piece together the complete story about the Maya civilization.

Those scientists wondered how the Maya built those magnificent cities and temples; how did they create such stunning pieces of art and jewelry? They tried to understand what the Maya drew, carved, and wrote on their walls and books. Every aspect of Maya life was interesting to them. As their research progressed and understanding and knowledge of the Maya civilization accumulated, one thing became clear to historians. The Maya were one of the most important and most influential civilizations of the whole Mesoamerican region. A simple illustration of that point is that if you were to close your eyes and try to imagine a general picture of Mesoamerican life prior to Columbus' so-called discovery of Americas, you would most likely see the quintessential representation of the Maya civilization. You might envision people walking around dressed in jaguar skins, or ones with brightly-colored headdresses made from feathers, or huge step pyramid temples adorned with strange hieroglyphic carvings, maybe people with painted faces and pierced noses and ears, human sacrifices in front of the masses, or warriors with wooden clubs sneaking across the jungle. We can't even imagine Mesoamerican history and culture without the Maya. And that is why it is rather important to know as much as we can about them.

In this book we will try to shine a bit of light on the Maya civilization, from its origins and history, through the everyday life of the Maya people, with the unavoidable topic of their religion and mythology, ending with the usually forgotten subject of what happened to the Maya after the Spaniards came and where are they now. And at the same time, with getting to know more about this important civilization, another important part of this book is to debunk some of the myths and misconceptions that, like with all other great civilizations, became synonymous with the Maya. So, get ready to learn and enjoy on this guided tour through Maya civilization.

Chapter 1 – Meet the Maya

Every story about the civilizations of the American continent begins around 40.000 to 20.000 years B.C.E., when during the last great Ice Age, a land bridge connected Alaska and Siberia. During that long period, small groups gradually started moving to what would be later named the New World by the European explorers. Although there have been some other theories about how and when the humans first migrated to the Americas, this theory is currently predominant thanks to abundant evidence that supports it. First, archeologists found similarity between the tools that were used by the people living in Siberia during that period and the tools of the first settlers across the Pacific Ocean. Then the linguists found core similarities and relations of the Siberian languages with the languages spoken by the Native Americans. The last and probably most conclusive piece of evidence came from geneticists, who compared DNA from both groups of people and found common ancestry. They confirmed that most of the indigenous people of the Americas came from what is today southeastern Siberia.

Of course, that migration didn't happen in one huge wave, but slowly, over time, small bands and tribes crossed over from Asia. And from Alaska and northern parts of America, they started migrating south. They did that as they searched for better places to live, with warmer climates with more diverse plant life and better hunting grounds. Over hundreds and thousands of years, these bands of hunters and gatherers roamed across the continent and started to adapt, inventing new more unique stone tools. Archeologists found those tools on the Yucatan peninsula, which is the Maya homeland, and they have dated it to around 10.000-8.000 B.C.E. That is probably when the first people, most likely Maya ancestors, came to the region. But before moving on to how those early hunter-gatherers rose to become the fabled Maya, we have to understand where they lived and how it affected the development of their early civilization.

So-called Maya homeland covered the southeastern parts of present-day Mexico, including the already mentioned Yucatan peninsula, and northwestern part of Central America, on territories of modern-day Belize and Guatemala, and parts of El Salvador and Honduras. From that, we can see that the Maya covered a relatively large area, around 320.000 km^2 (123.000 mi^2), which can be divided into three geographical and climate zones. To the north, covering pretty much the entire Yucatan peninsula are the Lowlands, then in the center of the Maya region are the Highlands, and in the south is the Pacific Coastal Plain. The Pacific coast region was a dense rainforest area, with the highest amounts of annual rainfall of the entire Maya homeland. Some of the first Maya settlements were founded in this region, along the lagoons on the coast. With plentiful forest wildlife and plants, sea and freshwater creatures it was a perfect place for early settlers, while the rich soils along the river banks made it a good place for agricultural societies that came later. It was also an important trade route in later periods when more complex communities arose, connecting Mexico and Central America.

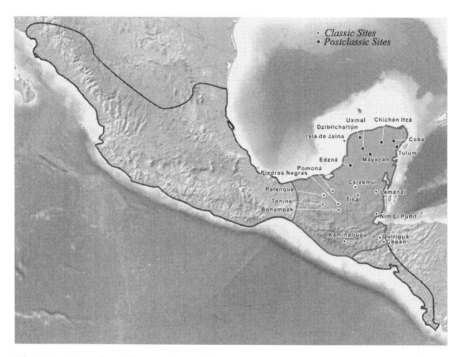

The Maya homeland. Source: https://commons.wikimedia.org

To the northeast of the Pacific coast region is the Highland region, aptly named for its high mountains of an average elevation of over 760m (2500ft), with highest peaks reaching up to about 3000m (9850ft). With higher altitude came lower temperatures as well as less rainfall. Yet the volcanic activity of the mountains provided important stone resources for the Maya like obsidian (also known as volcanic glass) and volcanic basalt. Volcanoes also made the surrounding soil quite fertile, and certain valleys climate was perfect for farming. Beside volcanic stones, the Highlands were also rich with other precious minerals like jade and serpentine. All that combined made this area favorable for settling despite the danger from volcanic eruptions and earthquakes. Quite different from that area are the Lowlands, which are mostly flat, and were in the past covered with thick forest. This region is rich with limestone and chert, important building materials for the Maya, as well with areas of fertile soil and abundant wildlife. Southern parts of the Lowlands are filled with lakes and rivers, which provided fish for the inhabitants, and at the same time facilitated communication throughout the dense forest. In northern areas, which are richer with limestone, water is more scarce, and the only sources of it were the sinkholes, also known as cenotes in that region. And the coast of the Atlantic Ocean on the Yucatan Peninsula provided this region with both saltwater fish and shellfish. When all things are considered, even if at the first glance it doesn't seem so, the whole Maya homeland was rather rich with food, water, and building materials, which explains why exactly the Maya ancestors chose to settle there.

But probably more important than that was the abundance of fertile soil. Around 6.000 B.C.E., agriculture spread around Mesoamerica, which marked a vital step in the development of the Maya culture. Their ancestors were already living somewhat sedentary lives, with an abundance of food in the forests around them. But with the rise of farming around 2000 B.C.E., they had more food surpluses, which meant the population grew faster and was more prosperous. And in search of the more fertile soils, the Maya ancestors started spreading from the coastal part of the Maya homeland inward, which explains why the Highlands were at first a bit slower in their development. As their societies became more complex, thanks partially to more excess food but also due to connections with other Mesoamerican civilizations, their cultures started to evolve, and around 1500 B.C.E. an early Maya civilization was beginning to form. Though it should be mentioned that linguists today believe that Proto-Mayan language, from which all modern Mayan languages evolved, formed as early as 2200 B.C.E., which meant that the Maya people had differentiated from other Mesoamerican tribes even before they rose to a level of civilization.

Of course, in the early stages of their development, the Maya were not as dominant as we usually depict them. From 1500 B.C.E. to around 250 C.E. there existed the early Maya civilization, known by historians as the Preclassic period. During this time, the Maya learned, adopting new technologies and ideas from their neighbors who were, at the time, more developed. Then came the Maya golden age, the Classic period, which lasted from about 250 to 950 C.E. In that era, also known as middle Maya civilization, they were the most dominant culture in Mesoamerica, with huge cities, a strong economy, advanced technology compared to others. But that golden age came quite abruptly to an end during the 10th century A.D., which led to the third era of the Maya – the late Maya civilization, or Postclassic period, which lasted until the Spaniards came to Mesoamerica in the early 16th century. That period is marked by a slow fall of the Maya, who were still an important civilization, but no longer as dominant as before. Of course, all that changed with the arrival of the Spaniards who had demonstrated little understanding of any culture, religion, or idea that didn't agree with their Christian view of the world. So, with great dedication, they worked on crushing the Maya people and their civilization, which led them to be mostly forgotten for a few centuries. They became just one more "savage" tribe from the so-called New World.

That attitude slowly started to change in the early 19th century when Mexico and other Central American countries gained independence from the crumbling Spanish Empire. Many became interested in the history of these lands, with their curiosity being sparked by some of the fine Maya artifacts that had been circulating in the art markets. Of course, at the time, the art collectors weren't aware that these were actually Maya artifacts. Yet some daring explorers started to roam the thick Mexican jungles, some in search of knowledge, others in search of material gain. Over the decades they found many sites covered with jungle trees and vines, gathering more attention which culminated in the 1890's when the first major archeological excavation and examination of the Maya sites began. By then archeologists and historians were sure that pre-Columbian civilizations, of which the Maya were probably the most famous one, were more than mere "barbarians," but now their task was to understand those cultures and uncover the past. Although many Maya sites were found and researched in the late 19th and early 20th century, not much was yet known about this mysterious civilization.

The 1950s marked a turning point in understanding the Maya past. Firstly, new technologies and new archeological sites allowed researchers to attain a more complex grasp of how the Maya civilization looked and evolved. But more important were the first breakthroughs in deciphering the Maya writing, which meant that researchers could gain a new level of comprehension of the Maya past. Understanding text written on monuments, in books, and on temple walls gave far more details about the Maya than any other artifact could. That groundbreaking discovery also ignited a new interest in the scholars about Maya history, making it one of the most dynamic fields of historic research at that time. Even today, new archeological findings are being uncovered and scholars have an even better understanding of Maya script, widening our knowledge and understanding of the Maya civilization. And today, as the interdisciplinary approach has become the norm in the discovery of the past, archeologists and historians are now working together with scientists from other fields, such as linguists, anthropologists, geneticists, which is important for getting a better, more detailed picture of the Maya civilization.

One of those details about the Maya that is rather important to know is that they aren't as unified as a group as most people imagine. When thinking about them, most people assume it is one big homogenous tribe that formed a civilization, perhaps similar to the ancient Greeks. But in reality, the Maya were more divided in smaller groups. This is most evident in their language, which from the early Proto-Mayan and over the course of thousands of years has split into many smaller regional language groups. By the time of the classical era of the Maya civilization, there were six large language subgroups of the Mayan; Yucatecan, Huastecan, Ch'olan-Tzeltalan, Q'anjob'alan, Mamean, and K'ichean. But despite those divisions among the Maya population, they surprisingly managed to keep a tight cultural and civilizational cohesion, similar to ancient Mesopotamian civilization. Of course, since the times of the classical Maya, much has changed, and today linguists have differentiated about 30 variations of the Mayan language. Of those languages most used is K'iche' (Quiché), with approximately 1 million speakers, concentrated in Guatemala. Also important is the Yucatec Maya language, which covers the largest area, the Yucatan peninsula, and has about 800,000 present-day speakers. Overall, there are more than 6 million people still speaking one of the many Mayan languages, although it should be mentioned that not all of them consider Mayan to be their first language.

A present-day Maya family from Yucatan, Mexico. Source:
https://commons.wikimedia.org

That leads us to another truth that is often overlooked when talking about the Maya; their history doesn't end in the 16th century, nor did they disappear as a unique ethnic group. Although Spanish rule heavily influenced them, they managed to keep their identity intact, preserving their language, traditions, and culture to the present day. Most of the Maya today live in Guatemala, where they constitute about 40% of the entire population. They also form a significant minority in southern Mexico and the Yucatan Peninsula. Honduras, Belize, and El Salvador also still have some indigenous Maya, but in much smaller numbers. Altogether there are somewhere between 6 and 7 million Maya people today, making them one of the larger native ethnic groups in Americas, which is another important reason for us to get to know more about their past, their culture, and their civilization.

Chapter 2 – From tribal villages to early states

Before going into the finer details about the Maya civilization we first must take a look at how it developed through history, starting with the earliest era, the Preclassic period. It is during this time that the Maya created the base of their culture, making their society more complex and changing their economy, warfare, and politics. Their civilization evolved from tribal villages, through more complex chiefdoms and resulted in the early Maya states. Those changes first began on the Pacific Coast region where, most likely thanks to the improvement of agriculture, the Maya first came to have food surpluses. By 1700 B.C.E., there were already some larger villages showing clear signs of a completely sedentary lifestyle, although rather primitive and uncivilized. But in the next century or so another great and important improvement began to appear. That improvement was pottery. As a cultural expression, it was used to make figurines which were mostly representations of females, as in most early societies around the world. In more practical forms, the Maya started making pottery vessels for storing and transporting food. It is important to note that this rise of sedentary agricultural life was happening at the similar time across Mesoamerica, which allowed for the development of trade. And, luckily for the Pacific coast Maya, they were in perfect position for it.

The easiest and quickest trade route from Central America to present-day Mexico crossed the Maya territory in the far south. And with pottery, it was easier to transport and trade food, which was most likely the first trading item of the region. For the Maya, like for many early civilizations, it was a crucial step in evolution. Trade sparked the stratification of the society, and the birth of the elite class among the Maya. Due to the gathering of wealth and power, the ruling strata started to exert increasing levels of control over the lower classes. This led to forming of the first so-called petty chiefdoms during 1400 B.C.E., in which a central village ruled small hamlets. These signs of hierarchical society meant that the early Maya chiefs were also able to force the commoners to take part in public works needed to create communal projects like building temples or other ritual buildings, which were the cornerstones of early civilizations. Further, trade pushed the Maya society to develop better craftsmanship and new tools, both to improve farming, for even more food surpluses, and also to be traded. That meant that besides farming, part of the Maya population focused on developing craftsmanship skills. And that social diversification is considered to be another important step in the creation of early civilizations.

Not long after, by the 1200s, the Maya villages on the Pacific coast became rich and powerful, with populations of more than 1000 for the first time. They improved their pottery to the artisanal levels, while large amounts of obsidian in some of those villages shows us that their wealth and power came from the control of that valuable resource. Yet trade remained the most important thing that drove the Maya civilization forward. At this point, the most developed Maya villages became powerful enough to evolve from local to regional trade, which meant the Maya came in contact with other higher developed societies. Of these, the most significant was probably the Olmecs that lived on the Gulf Coast of south-central Mexico. The Olmecs were at the time the most developed civilization, with structured religion, trade, urban centers, and highly sophisticated art; they are considered to have influenced the development of the entire family of Mesoamerican cultures and civilizations. The Maya were no exception. From the Olmecs, the Maya adopted the base of their future civilization, from the pantheon of gods and monumental buildings to urbanism and rituals, and to art style and veneration of rulers.

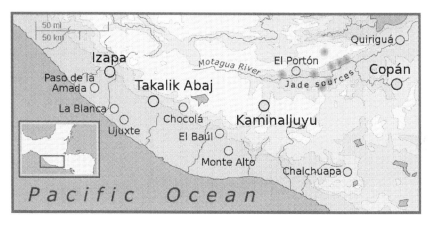

Pacific coast region of the Maya homeland. Source:
https://commons.wikimedia.org

But even though the signs of cultural interaction of the Olmecs with a large part of Mesoamerica is certain, in recent years there have been some historians that tend to disagree with the notion of the Olmec civilization being mother culture of the entire region. They believe that the cultural exchange happened so quickly it is impossible to be sure if all the traits mentioned actually originate from the Olmecs. They argue that this civilizational leap is work of the entire network of the Mesoamerican cultures, connected through trade. But no one can deny that during that early era of Mesoamerican history the Olmec cities were the biggest and most powerful, and many of their neighbors and trading partners copied from them. Among those mimicking the Olmecs were clearly at least some of the Maya villages. By 1000 B.C.E., Olmec-styled art began to replace earlier forms of the Maya figurines and vessels, while jade became an important precious material coveted by the Maya elite. Later on, from around 850 B.C.E., when those villages started to grow into urban centers, they also mimicked the configuration of La Venta, the most important and the mightiest Olmec city from 900 to 300 B.C.E.

That leap from villages to early cities is important; it indicates that by the time Maya civilization had become richer and more powerful, it was at least in part thanks to their increased trade with the Olmecs and other cultures. But this was only the state of affairs in the Pacific Coast region of the Maya homeland. In the north, in the Lowlands, things were slightly different. During the time the southern Maya started to get involved in the regional trade, around 1200 B.C.E., their northern brethren remained at the low level of simple agricultural villages and still lived in egalitarian society. The lowland Maya started to catch up with the Pacific Coast around 1000 B.C.E., as the first signs of public architecture show us. This meant that society was getting stratified, while the Olmec-style jade artwork shows us that they slowly started to get involved in the trade as well. By 700 B.C.E., the changes in the lowland Maya societies started to pick up the pace as their population started to grow faster. They started to create monumental public complexes, while they also worked on making ridged and drained fields for farming. And trade became a more vital part of their lives, similar to the southern Maya. The artifacts found in the lowland Maya centers are mostly of Olmec origin, which shows that they were one of the most important trade partners of the lowland area as well.

As both southern and northern parts regions of the Maya homeland experienced a period of growth, accumulation of wealth and power, the strongest cities started to evolve from previously mentioned petty chiefdoms to proto-states. One of the earliest and best examples of this is the La Blanca site, which flourished roughly from 900 to 600 B.C.E., in the Pacific Coast region. It managed to gain control of 300km^2 (115mi^2) of the territory around it, with two more urban centers apart from the capital. Those centers were of course smaller, and hierarchically secondary to the capital. Alongside these urban centers, La Blanca inhabitants controlled at least 60 smaller villages and hamlets in the surrounding area. That kind of power granted La Blanca a lot of labor power, which was used in monumental public works. One of the examples of that mobilization of the workforce was a platform temple that was 24m (78ft) high and is considered to be one of the largest in Mesoamerica of that era. Apart from La Blanca, many other similar larger urban centers spawned in the southernmost parts of the Maya region, with a more complex site hierarchy and influence than in earlier times.

One of the most illuminating examples of this power comes from the ruler tombs in these capitals. The biggest tomb, dated to about 500 B.C.E., was a stone crypt, that was filled with precious goods like jade and shells, a carved stone scepter and three trophy heads which were a clear indicator of status and wealth of the male buried in it. But more than that, the true power wielded by the dead king was demonstrated by the 12 human sacrifices found around him. They, unlike the king, were buried with their faces down. Their role in this burial ritual was most likely to be servants to the ruler in his afterlife. Human sacrifices and trophy heads also show us, together with other carvings and findings of projectile heads, that warfare was becoming a more important and regular part of the Maya life. The Maya rulers found that small-scale raids were a good way to both gain wealth and labor force, but also to eliminate their rivals. Besides that, war captives were used for religious sacrifices, and with that rituals rulers also reinforced authority over their subordinates, proving that they are more than capable of taking care of them in both religious and material aspects of life.

The prosperity of the material and religious life was also evident in the Lowland region, although not as much as on the Pacific Coast. They erected even larger temples than before, like ones in the south Lowland site of El Mirador, which rivaled in size the Egyptian pyramids. They also built ritual ball courts as well as *sacbeob,* singular *sacbe,* which were elevated roadways connecting temples, plazas, and other structures in ceremonial sites which most likely had some religious significance. Yet at this time it seems that the most important process in the Lowlands was the expansion of the Maya from riversides and lakes into the much densely forested interior of the region. This was made possible by development of swidden agriculture, more widely known as the slash-and-burn technique, which made it possible to clear parts of the forest for farming, then leaving it to replenish so the process could be repeated. With that expansion, nearly all of the entire Lowland region was now settled by the Maya people.

The expansion of Maya civilization was not only limited to the Lowlands. As both northern and southern areas of Maya territory got wealthier and more involved in trade, they also spread their influence to the Highlands. Of course, this mountain region was settled as early as 1000 B.C.E., but it remained fairly sparsely developed. Their growth and expansion only stated around 800 B.C.E., most likely influenced by the development of trade between the Lowlands and the Pacific Coast, which meant traders had to cross over the Highlands. This meant the Highland Maya started to learn and adopt advances made by their kinfolk. By 600 B.C.E., they started to use irrigation to make the valleys they lived in more fertile, and this with other signs of public works like monuments and temples show that by that time they had managed to develop stratified societies where elites were able to mobilize the labor force for common projects. The best example of that is Kaminaljuyu, an urban center located in present-day central Guatemala, near Guatemala City, which managed to use the control of irrigation to enforce its direct rule over the entire valley in which it was built. Carvings show that the rulers of this city exerted strong authority thanks to their religious roles as well as their success in warfare. And, as they were located on an important trade route that connected the south and north Maya regions, they got quite wealthy by controlling it.

Of course, that wealth was going mostly to the ruling elite, or to be more precise to the rulers, as was the case in nearly all Mesoamerican cities at the time. This accumulation of wealth and power in the hands of the rulers was the key for the next step of development in the Maya society, which was forming of the early states. But by 400 B.C.E., cities like previously mentioned

Kaminaljuyu and El Mirador, as well as many others, grew considerably, covering up to a 4km² (1.5mi²), which made these urban centers as big, if not bigger than, cities of Ancient Greece like Athens. That growth was a direct consequence of their success in trade, as the previously dominant Olmecs were in steady decline, slowly disappearing from the historical stage. With more wealth, the Maya society became more stratified, with more than just two classes-the ruling elites and the commoners. All that culminated with the creation of a strong ruler cult, possibly influenced by the Olmecs, which was partially based on their religious role in the society. With the unquestionable authority of the rulers, which can by now be even called kings, the transformation of the Maya polities from chiefdoms to states was complete.

An excavated portion of the Kaminaljuyu acropolis. Source:
https://commons.wikimedia.org

A good example of this transformation is El Ujuxte, a city that can in a way be considered a successor of La Blanca as the most important urban center of the Pacific Coast region. That power center managed to form a state that covered a 600km^2 (230mi^2) area, with four levels of administrative hierarchy, ranging from a few dozen simple, smaller villages, to secondary city centers that copied the capital. And as the capital, El Ujuxte itself was centrally-organized with large monumental buildings at the city core, which most likely filled ceremonial and religious roles that were also important for the authority of the ruler. That center was surrounded by the residential area, which meant that this city was a busy urban center with a lively economy. The archeologists think that this state, besides controlling trade routes on the coast, which was certainly a huge part of its success, relied on cacao and rubber as main resources that made it wealthy. Of course, the riches that were flowing into the city were mostly going to the ruler and the elite around him, which is evidenced by the numerous grand public works, tombs, and monuments the kings built as signs of their power. Of course, El Ujuxte wasn't a lone example for this, there were many states and cities on the Pacific Coast that went through similar growth and advance in the last centuries before the common era.

The northern Maya of the Lowlands also followed similar development, which is probably most evident at the El Mirador archeological site. The city of El Mirador was slightly smaller than El Ujuxte, but its true power is clearly shown through the scale of its monumental buildings. La Danta pyramid temple, which was part of this urban center, wasn't only the biggest pyramid in the history of the entire Maya civilization, but it also holds the title of the biggest known pyramid in all of Mesoamerica. Furthermore, being 72m (236ft) high with an estimated volume of 2,800,000 cubic meters, it is one of the biggest pyramids in the whole world. And, even though the majestic temple remains impressive for its time as well as our own, it is worth noting that much more labor in the form of construction and maintenance went to the network of roads and causeways that connected El Mirador with its subordinate centers. Those pathways made trade much easier and allowed the rulers of this state to control it better. Similarly to El Ujuxte, that control was the backbone of El Mirador's power and wealth. But unfortunately, even though there are clear signs that some of the surrounding towns and villages were under control of El Mirador, archeologists cannot be exactly sure how far and wide its political dominance reached. What is certain is that the authority of the El Mirador kings was enormous, especially for that time, commanding thousands of laborers and ruling over a population that measured in tens of thousands. Without a doubt, they ruled over the most powerful state in the Lowlands.

The kings of Kaminaljuyu were in a rather similar position to their peers of El Mirador and El Ujuxte, ruling over a state that was the most powerful in the Highland region. Exact hierarchy and reach of its direct rule are today uncertain, due to the fact that the present-day Guatemala City lies on a large portion of that ancient metropolis. Yet, with signs of control over important obsidian quarries located about 19km (11mi) northeast of Kaminaljuyu, it can be seen clearly that its political dominance covered a rather large area. But, the control of those quarries also reveals that this city was an important producing center of cutting tools, which were exported to other areas of the Maya homeland. Besides its own exports, the economy of the Kaminaljuyu was also dependent on the trade connection between the Lowlands and the Pacific Coast which went over its territory. With the rising economy, the rulers of that city were able to expand earlier irrigation systems with two new large canals, which was important for advancing the agriculture in the area not so well suited for it. That kind of public projects also clearly shows that the Kaminaljuyu kings also excreted rather strong authority over their subordinates, as manpower needed to build and later maintain that irrigation systems, as well as other monumental building, was equal to manpower used by El Mirador rulers needed for their public works. Beside that indirect evidence of their power and wealth, numerous monuments and richly filled tombs also stand as testimony to that.

But those monuments tell more than just how mighty various rulers and kings were. They also give a glimpse of how with the development of states the Maya society also became more complex. Looking at those monuments, as well as other pieces of art, it is clear there were more specialized artisans, who focused more on honing their skills to new levels. That kind of horizontal stratification of the society is the result of a more diverse division of labor and developed economy. One of the products of that the evolved Maya society was cultural and civilizational development, which led to some significant innovations. The most influential and most important of those were certainly the development of writing systems and now so-called Mayan calendar. Though it is true both of those innovations were actually adopted from other Mesoamerican civilizations, with them the Maya developed all the hallmarks of what we today consider to be their classical civilization. Some historians even consider this period, around 1st century B.C.E. and 1st century C.E. should be seen more as an early Classic period rather than late Preclassic, but the old division remains. But no matter how scientists label this period, it is clear that the Maya society achieved rather high levels of sophistication.

Unfortunately, that sophistication doesn't mean the Maya were peaceful, neither among themselves nor towards their neighbors. This is clearly evident from scenes of conquests and victories of the Maya kings and warriors, which were a common topic of carvings on monuments, as well as some other types of arts. Human sacrifices and trophy heads show not only the militant side of the Maya society, but also that prowess in war was important for cementing authority of the Maya kings. And if all that seems like circumstantial evidence, the fact that some of those rulers built fortified ditches and walls around their cities undoubtedly confirms that war was an important part of Maya society. And it seems none were safe from the dangers of war, no matter how strong and big their states were, as even El Mirador, one of the most powerful cities at the time, was fortified. Archeologists have also found signs of struggle on some sites, which have signs of deliberate destruction, showing that warfare didn't consist only consist of simple plundering raids, but was actually aimed at destroying the enemy at times. But wars didn't only affect the two, or more, sides that were involved directly in fighting. Some cities suffered greatly when clashes for power disrupted important trade, which obviously was an important part of the Maya economy.

Some historians even argue that it was war that was the root cause of the decline of the early Maya civilization that began around 150 C.E. They think that competition for power and control of trade actually disrupted it so much that many cities were abandoned and destroyed, leading to a so-called cultural hiatus that approximately lasted from 150 to 250 C.E. But although war clearly played an important part in demise of the preclassic Maya, it is more likely that this was brought about by a set of interconnected circumstances. For one, there is evidence of droughts in nearly the entire Maya homeland. It is thought that the humans themselves played a crucial part in causing that with overpopulation, deforestation, and the overuse of fertile soil. This led to drying out of lakes around Kaminaljuyu, while El Mirador surroundings turned into a swampy area. And as if that wasn't enough, Ilopango volcano in El Salvador erupted on the edges of the southern region around 200 C.E. Many sites on the southeast were abandoned; ones which were important producers of obsidian tools, vital for the Maya economy, and which cut off the trade routes to Pacific Coast cities and the rest of Central America. And volcanic ash that spread around the region made farming much more difficult, clogging the rivers and changing their courses.

Those natural disasters more largely affected the Pacific Coast region, which led to the fact that it lost its place as the most developed region of the Maya civilization, ceding that role to the Lowlands. Disruption of trade in the south yielded new possibilities for the northern Maya, which they took. Yet these weren't enough to save all of them, and El Mirador fell since the swampland wasn't fertile enough to maintain its large population. Kaminaljuyu was of a mixed fortune. The city survived, although it seems that a new group of the western Mesoamericans took control of it, which is another sign of an upsurge in wars at the period. The natural disasters led to dwindling resources, which prompted much fiercer competition for them, leading to an escalation of war between the Maya states. All these factors combined led not only to cultural hiatus and power shift from south to north but to a major depopulation of the entire Maya region as well, leading to further weakening of the Maya civilization. But no matter how disastrously the Preclassic period of the Maya history ended, it was an important period that established the basics of their civilization, which remained in place until the final demise of the Maya during the Spanish conquest.

Chapter 3 – The Golden age

So-called hiatus of the Maya civilization that occurred in the late Preclassic era, no matter how apocalyptical the accounts of it sound, didn't actually mean the end of the Maya story. That period was more of a pause in development and blossoming of the Maya. The biggest consequence was that the Pacific Coast region lost its place as the most advanced region, leaving that title to the southern Lowlands. That area became the heart of the Classic period, marking the apex of the Maya civilization. Many changes occurred, mostly building on the foundations laid in previous centuries. Rulers weren't only seen as connected to the gods through ceremonies and rituals, but were venerated themselves. And Classic-era rulers were now depicted usually wearing warrior outfits, symbolizing their evolution to warrior-kings. Writing spread, but remained focused on religious and state affairs, while the temples were still the center of public life. Maya art became more colorful and detailed, reaching new levels of finesse. This golden age allowed also the Maya population to rise substantially, yet the political landscape never allowed them to unify into a single empire. This left the civilization split into many states which managed to outshine and dwarf the states of the early Maya civilization.

As almost all aspects of the Maya classic era had their roots in the previous age, so did most cities and states. Tikal, a major power of the middle Maya civilization situated in northern Guatemala, was no exception. It was one of the cities that managed to benefit from the fall of El Mirador which dominated part of the Maya homeland, leading to Tikal becoming an important trading hub that connected east and west Mesoamerica. The political power of this state was apparent, as it managed to take control of surrounding cities, and install allied dynasties in cities that were further away, in present-day Yucatan or Honduras. The city of Tikal itself grew to levels unimaginable to the Maya of the Preclassic era. It covered an area of 60km^2 (23mi^2), but even more impressive is the fact that the city fortifications defended an area of 123km^2 (48mi^2). The population of this huge city is estimated to have been between 60 and 100 thousand people, which is another sign of its power and wealth. By 300 C.E., Tikal grew so powerful that it established not only trade, but diplomatic connections to Central Mexico, making it the mightiest state of the early classic age.

Of course, the Tikal kings, as all previous Maya rulers, wanted to mark their success and power. They did that on monuments, or to be more precise, on stelae. They carved important dates and names on them in celebration of themselves, subsequently leaving behind some of the most important sources historians today have about the era. On one of them, a founding ruler of this city is marked as Yax Ehb Xook, who ruled around the 1st century C.E. Historians are certain he wasn't the first ruler, since the city was founded way before that, so they assume he garnered the title of "founder" for helping to achieve political independence. These monuments demonstrate how Tikal ended the independence of the cities around it, since in conquered cities, there are no traces of stelae dedicated to local rulers. One of the most interesting stories that we can see from these monuments is a dynastic change in Tikal. In 378 C.E. a king named Chak Tok Ich'aak I (Jaguar Paw) died when Siyaj K'ak' (Smoking Frog) arrived in the city. If at first, that seems like a coincidence, the fact that next king, Yax Nuun Ayiin (Curl Nose), was crowned a year later by Siyaj K'ak' clearly shows it wasn't. That takeover wasn't peaceful, as most of the stelae built before 378 were defaced and vandalized. Also, it appears that Yax Nuun Ayiin didn't claim the throne by any signs of legitimacy, as records show he claimed to be a son of a ruler of an unspecified kingdom.

Central Plaza and the temple in Tikal. Source: https://commons.wikimedia.org

Although the exact origin of Curl Nose isn't stated on the monuments, historians narrowed it down to the one, almost certain candidate – the city of Teotihuacan, in Central Mexico, later Aztec region. Evidence for that lies that sources indicate that Smoking Frog and his army came from that direction, but also because Yax Nuun Ayiin is shown adorned as a Teotihuacano. Of course, that proof isn't completely conclusive, but the fact that Teotihuacan was one of the largest and most powerful cities in all of Mesoamerica, dominating from 1st to 6th century C.E., also supports that theory. The might and reach of the city were so big that some historians even argued its rise was one of the disruptive factors in Maya trade that caused the Maya hiatus. But it is important to note that around 400 C.E., the Central American "superpower" Teotihuacan also installed its vassal allies in Kaminaljuyu, which, combined with control of Tikal, meant that Teotihuacan obtained more direct access to prestige resources like jade, obsidian, jaguar pelts, and tropical bird feathers. This interaction between two regions also influenced the Maya culture as well, influencing their art style, architecture, and other aspects of their civilization. Teotihuacano conquerors also brought their more advanced and lethal weapons, which were quickly adopted by the Maya, while this foreign influence also helped the rise of warrior-king symbolism and its cult, which was already established in the Central Mexican region.

The influence of Teotihuacan wasn't limited just to culture; it impacted the economy and politics as well. Being an ally of the most powerful state in the region, and part of its extensive ally network was certainly beneficial to Tikal. Access to much greater resources through Teotihuacan's trade network made Tikal far richer than before, making its economy the strongest in the early Classic period of the Maya civilization. At the same time, an alliance with the Mesoamerican powerhouse raised the political influence of Tikal, making it the mightiest state of the period in the Lowlands, and subsequently the entire Maya homeland. A strong economy coupled with political might, of course, led to military expansion. Some cities, like nearby Uaxactun, Tikal incorporated directly in its kingdom through direct control. Ones that were further away like Copan, located in present-day western Honduras, had their dynasties overthrown and substituted by rulers loyal to Tikal. So, suffering a fate similar to Tikal, those states were also put in a sort of vassal position to their power center. But, by achieving such dominance, Tikal made a lot of enemies, who were likely opposed to both its economic and political supremacy, as well to the foreign factor in their rule and culture. That is why slowly an anti-Tikal alliance, led by the city of Calakmul, was being formed.

Calakmul was a city located in present-day southeastern Mexico, near the border with Guatemala, 38km (24 mi) north of El Mirador. And similarly to Tikal, it controlled part of the trade routes that went through the Lowlands. At its height, the city had an estimated population of 50 to 100 thousand people, living in a $20km^2$ ($8mi^2$) area surrounded by a network of canals and reservoirs which, to a certain extent, served as fortified protection from outside attack. The early history of Calakmul is not known, but some evidence has its origins in the late Preclassic period and connects its first dynastic ruler with El Mirador. But by 500 C.E., it became powerful enough to challenge Tikal's supremacy, and Calakmul rulers started building alliances with states that surrounded their enemy. The biggest diplomatic success was turning Caracol, formerly Tikal's ally, to their side during mid-6th century. This city was founded in the late Preclassic or early Classic period in what is today western Belize. In that earliest period, there are signs of central Mexican influence, making it a part of Teotihuacan's trade network. At the time of confrontation with Tikal, it was a rising city, which at the height of its power had about 100 to 120 thousand people covering over 100km^2 (38mi^2).

The confrontation between Calakmul and Tikal started in the 530s when Tikal's allies managed to defeat Calakmul. But that defeat wasn't total as, by the end of the decade, Calakmul recovered. The major turning point came in 553 C.E. when Lord Water from Caracol switched sides and allied with Calakmul. Though Tikal, under Wak Chan K'awiil, managed to achieve the first victory in 556 C.E., it wasn't enough to end the war. When Sky Witness was crowned as the king of Calakmul around 561, fortunes changed. Historians think that he orchestrated the defeat of Tikal in 562 C.E. by the hands of Lord Water, who in his raid on the enemy also managed to capture Wak Chan K'awiil. The Tikal ruler was sacrificed, but the war lasted with lessened intensity for about another decade, concluding with a complete loss of Tikal. There are many reasons why this powerful state wasn't able to come out of this war was as a victor. For one, during this period Teotihuacan started to decline, partially because of the draughts, but there are signs of a military defeat there as well. Secondly, during its supremacy, Tikal acted in such a way that it alienated most of the other Maya states, so it couldn't count on wide support from its neighbors. And finally, it seems Calakmul was able to impact its trade, weakening its material power so vital in waging war.

In the end, for Tikal, the loss didn't mean just loss of wealth and power. It marked the end of its independence for roughly 130 years. Its rulers were subjugated to the kings of Calakmul, who didn't allow them to build any monuments and stelae. Most of the city's financial gain went to their new master as a tribute and, as a result, the population growth in Tikal stopped. That period of suppression of this former major Maya power is now called Tikal's hiatus, during which there weren't any advances in the city. Of course, this wasn't limited only to Tikal. For example, in Uaxactun, which was under Tikal's control, building completely stopped during this period, and the hiatus spread over many cities that were subjugated by Tikal. Logically the biggest winner of this war was Calakmul, which gained a lot of political power, expanded its area of control, and, without Tikal as trade competition, prospered. Caracol was also boosted by the defeat of its former ally, experiencing tremendous growth in population and size, as well as in economy. But unfortunately for the Maya, this war didn't bring permanent peace to the region.

With Tikal gone from the political scene of the Maya civilization, a great vacuum in power was left which Calakmul wasn't able to fill on its own. Its rulers managed to exploit the victory, and the city gained a lot, but they didn't manage to convert their military alliance in more permanent political domination over other Maya states. Their allies decided to resist Calakmul's authority and maintain their independence. And many cities, including Calakmul's allies, grew during the power vacuum. This led to more Maya states being able to compete against each other in competition for political influence and control of trade. That kind of political landscape brought a long period of wars and fighting among the Maya, which marks the transition from the early Classic to the late Classic period of this civilization. And even though escalation of warfare marked this era, Maya civilization actually prospered. This was a period of cultural growth, with advances in astronomical knowledge and the calendar, art sophistication, and even wider use of texts displaying new levels of scribe skills. The constant war didn't dampen the tremendous growth in the Maya population, which peaked at about 10 million. But, the elite class did use the continuous struggle to expand their power and control over the commoners, while at the same time extending sizes of their states to new levels. And as Teotihuacan fell, the Maya became the most developed civilization of Mesoamerica, spreading its art style and influence across the region.

At the beginning of the late Classic period, in the late 6th and early 7th century, Calakmul and Caracol continued to expand their power, attacking other states, conquering them, or creating vassal states from them. It seemed their supremacy was unquestioned. But almost constant wars took their toll, and their power was no longer unquestionable. As they weakened, kings of Tikal managed to regain part of its vitality. During the 640s C.E., A side branch of Tikal's royal family settled a new city, Dos Pilas, to serve as both a military and trade outpost. It was located 105km (65mi) to the southwest, in the region of Petexbatún Lake. As expected, Calakmul wasn't going to allow this without a fight, and in 659 they attacked Dos Pilas, defeating it most likely without much trouble. The ruler of that city, B'alaj Chan K'awiil, managed to escape execution and became a vassal of Yuknoom the Great, the Calakmul king. Yuknoom, in a rather smart political move, turned his new vassal against its former allies, putting two branches of Tikal royal dynasty into direct conflict. But even though Dos Pilas had a powerful ally, in 672 C.E., Tikal managed to take back the control of its former colony. Calakmul intervened five years later to reinstate B'alaj Chan K'awiil on the throne, driving away the occupying forces. And, as it was obvious to Yuknoom the Great that his ally and vassal wasn't able to fight Tikal on his own, in 679 C.E., he helped him to achieve a decisive victory over his own family. Although texts at Dos Pilas talk about piles of heads and pools of blood, this confrontation between old enemies showed that even though Calakmul was still the most powerful Maya state, it wasn't untouchable.

Another shock to the supremacy of Calakmul was when in the 680's two of its allies, Caracol and Naranjo, started a war between them. Naranjo was a city, also located in northern Guatemala, which suffered a lot from the clashes for supremacy between other larger states. In the beginning, it was an ally of Tikal, then it was taken by

Calakmul, and in the early 7th century it switched hands from Caracol and Calakmul. Yet Naranjo somehow managed to gain independence in 680 C.E., and then used the opportunity to settle the ongoing feud it had with Caracol. Yuknoom the Great decided to support Caracol, probably since it was an older ally, and managed to crush Naranjo's resistance. It would be expected of him to incorporate Naranjo back under his direct control, so he married the daughter of the Dos Pilas ruler to a Naranjo noble to restore dynasty in that city. Historians aren't in agreement as to why he did that, but the move actually managed to strengthen Naranjo, and during next couple of years it raided and attacked Caracol's territory. Calakmul's ability to control its allies and vassals was clearly fading, which was only worsened by the death of its eminent and successful king, Yuknoom the Great, in 686. C.E.

Tikal's new king Jasaw Chan K'awiil, who was crowned in 682 C.E., decided to exploit Calakmul's weakness. First, he strengthened his position in his own city, building new temples and stelae, erecting the first monument with the name of the ruler after Tikal's major defeat 6th century. It was him who brought Tikal out of so-called hiatus. With the restored prestige of his dynasty, in 695 C.E., he first attacked Naranjo, and later that same year he fought against Calakmul directly. In both battles he won, managing to capture a lot of prisoners who were later sacrificed. Historians aren't certain what happened the Calakmul's king, as there are some vague and unclear references to him being among the captured, but even if he managed to escape death at the hands of Jasaw Chan K'awiil, he soon vanished from the political stage. On the other hand, Tikal's king ruled for roughly another 40 years, completely renewing the power and status of his state. He managed to retake supremacy over the Maya states from Calakmul, but the rivalry between these two Maya "superpowers" continued for well over 100 years, through the late Classical period.

Even though Calakmul suffered a major defeat, Dos Pilas remained its ally. But it was no longer a subjugated vassal, as its growth in strength secured its independence. Heirs of B'alaj Chan K'awiil, who died soon after Yuknoom the Great, continued to spread their influence and territories through war and marriage. They managed to create what historians today call the Petexbatún Kingdom. In 735 C.E., Dos Pilas rulers managed to conquer Seibal, the largest city in their region, and by 741, the Petexbatún Kingdom had an area of 4000km^2 (1544 mi^2) under its control. With that expansion Dos Pilas also gained control of trade routes that went into the highlands, giving them a significant economic boost. From that quick success, it was likely that this kingdom would grow enough to compete for supremacy with Tikal and Calakmul, but its fortunes quickly changed. The city was attacked by their local enemies, who were fueled with revenge. Rulers of the Petexbatún Kingdom tried to defend their capital by quickly fortifying it, sacrificing their palaces and monuments to build walls, but it was futile, and in 761 C.E., Dos Pilas was ransacked. Petexbatún managed to survive, switching to another capital, and the war raged on with such ferocity that by 800's much of the region was abandoned, as people moved to safer places. By then. through constant warfare and destruction, Petexbatún Kingdom was dissolved.

One of the factors that contributed to the fall of Petexbatún is the fact that during 740s its mighty ally Calakmul suffered yet another defeat by Tikal. The cause for another clash was Calakmul's incentive to the city of Quiriguá to rebel against Copan, an old Tikal's ally. The city of Copan during the 7th century C.E. managed to expand its prestige and power, covering a sizable area in what is today western Honduras. At the height of its power in the early 8th century, one of Copan's kings even proclaimed it was politically equal to both Tikal and Calakmul, as well as Palenque, a city which we'll talk more about later in the chapter. Under control of that mighty Copan state was a much smaller city of Quiriguá, located about 50km (31mi) to the north of the capital. It was an important outpost for Copan as it allowed it to control jade trade as well as fertile valley around it. In 736 C.E. Calakmul's ruler met with his peer in Quiriguá, most likely giving him his support to rebel against Copan, which happened two years later. With new power behind it, Quiriguá managed to win its independence from its former masters and became an independent state, now connected to Calakmul. Copan lost economically important territory, and although it was never subdued by Quiriguá, it started to lose its prestige and might. On the other hand, Quiriguá managed to expand its power and wealth, becoming to some extent more powerful than its southern foe. That kind of meddling in its ally's affairs wasn't something Tikal could allow to go unpunished. So, in retaliation, Tikal attacked and conquered El Perú-Waḳa in 743 and Naranjo 744 C.E., these settlements being Calakmul's important allies and trade partners. That loss weakened Calakmul even further, and it never managed to regain its former glory. In contrast, Tikal once again gained complete control of east-west trade through the Lowlands, becoming yet again the unquestionable, number-one power of the Maya world.

Putting aside for a moment the struggle between Tikal and Calakmul, which seems to be the central political and economic problem of the late Classic era of the Maya civilization, there is another major city deserving of mention. That is Palenque, located in the western lowlands, the present-day southeastern Mexican state of Chiapas. Being on the edge of the Maya region, surrounded mostly by non-Maya tribes, Palenque managed for most of its history to remain uninvolved in the fight between the two Maya "superpowers." It was founded in the mid-5th century C.E., along a trade route that connected central Mexico and the Maya homeland. As such it was most likely part of Teotihuacan's trade network and at some point, an ally of Tikal. That is the only reason why Calakmul would have attacked a city that is 227km (150mi) away two times. Those demonstrations of Calakmul's power happened in 599 and 611 C.E., during Tikal's hiatus, and were the only extent of Palenque's direct involvement in the Tikal-Calakmul fight. Later, during the 7th century, Palenque flourished and managed to become a respectable and mighty state in the west, attacking and conquering a lot of its neighbors. But at the beginning of the next century its power started to waver, and in 711 and 764 C.E., it suffered two major defeats from an enemy state in their region.

It is clear that Palenque didn't play such a significant role in Maya politics, as it was on the margins of their world, but it is important for the historians. The reason for that is the culture and art that its citizens left behind. Palenque boasted some of the finest architectural work in the middle Maya civilization with elegant temples and, for that time, inventive vaulting techniques. Their artisans were masters of portraiture in stucco and Palenque kings left lengthy texts about their rule. And in those inscriptions, they don't write only about dynastic successions and wars, but also about their mythology. Because of that, they contain most vivid examples of how the Maya kings used legends, history, and religious beliefs to support their status and power. So even though the city of Palenque was smaller, politically weaker and less significant, it was culturally at least equal, if not superior, to both Calakmul and Tikal.

The Palace at Palenque with the aqueduct on the right. Source:
https://commons.wikimedia.org

That, of course, doesn't mean that other Maya cities and states were culturally undeveloped. The period between roughly 600 and 800 C.E., was the Maya golden age that gave rise to many technological achievements and artistic accomplishments; many great cities were built, and the population blossomed. And those achievements are evident in all Maya states, especially the wealthiest ones. Yet as the 9th century came to a close, the major polities started to collapse. As we have seen from examples of Palenque and Copan, their previous vassals rebelled against them, challenging their supremacy. The same happened to Tikal and Calakmul as well, and large kingdoms of the Classic Maya started to fragment into smaller polities. It was the first signs that glory days of the Maya were passing. One reason for the decline was that central dynasties were getting weaker, while the local elites were getting stronger, which could have been caused by almost constant wars that lasted for two centuries. The warfare certainly exhausted the wealth and might of the dynasties, making them more and more dependent on their subordinate elites, while the elites themselves at times gained a lot through fighting.

But the fall of the Classic Maya states didn't end with just loss of their territories and former vassals. By the mid-10th century, most of them had collapsed completely, being no longer centers of power. Some of the cities were totally abandoned, while others regressed into small villages with only a small agricultural population. Historians were for a long time uncertain how and why the Classic Maya civilization collapsed, arguing that it could have been brought about by droughts, overpopulation, wars, and uprisings or foreign invasions. Today it seems that the cause was actually all of those together. Political turmoil and fighting undermined trade and dynasties lost their power, while overpopulation of the central region combined with droughts, and overuse of soil led to food shortages. And one by one, southern Lowland cities were abandoned. As mentioned before, the Petexbatún region was abandoned by the 800s, and in other cities, the last inscribed monument is taken as the circa time they fell, since it is a clear sign of their loss of power and wealth. Those monuments are dated to 799 in Palenque, 810 in Calakmul, 820 in Naranjo and in Copan, 822 C.E. Caracol and Tikal lasted a bit longer, as their last monuments are dated to 849 and 869 C.E., respectively. With their fall, the golden age and so-called Late Classic Maya period ended.

Chapter 4 – From the golden age to the age of disaster

The fall of the southern Lowland cities, which were the most advanced in the Maya homeland, would have seemed to indicate that their civilization was also disappearing. Yet that was not the case. Their collapse only meant that the centers of power shifted to northern Lowlands, or to be more precise, to the Yucatan Peninsula. In that area there were many old Maya cities, some even dating back to the late Preclassic era, which profited from the downfall of the southern Lowland trade centers. These cities quickly seized the chance, becoming an important factor in trade connections between central Mexico and Central America. As those cities continued the traditions of the Classical Maya civilization, which clearly was in decline, historians refer to this new period as the Terminal Classic era. Another reason for that name is that during this period, the classical culture of the Maya civilization went through a change, and by the mid-10th century it had evolved into a new, more pan-Mesoamerican culture. The best example of the entire era and the changes that occurred during it is no other than probably the most famous Maya city today, Chichén Itzá.

The city of Chichén Itzá was located in the arid north of the Yucatan Peninsula, near two large limestone sinkholes or cenotes, explaining the translation of its name "the wells of the Itza." Its rise to prominence started during the Late Classic period thanks to trade, as the area wasn't as fertile as the southern Lowlands. Chichén Itzá, like many other Yucatan Maya states, used the maritime type of trade that went around the peninsula as the base of its economy. Of course, that maritime trade existed for a long time before the Terminal Classic period, but with political turmoil and disappearing trade routes in the southern Lowlands, it gained in importance. Another important factor that helped the expanse of this type of trade was a rise of new powers in Central Mexico that had arisen after the fall of Teotihuacan. By the Terminal period, this route connected the Gulf Coast of Mexico, which offered volcanic ash, obsidian, and jade, to Costa Rica and Panama which were rich with copper, silver, and gold. In between, the northern Maya offered fish, cotton, hemp rope, and honey. But the most important commodity of the Yucatan was high-quality salt, which coincidentally was the main resource traded by Chichén Itzá. This city annually exported 3,000 to 5,000 metric tons of it. But what is more impressive is the fact that Chichén Itzá is far away from the coast. To participate in trade the rulers of this city built and fortified a harbor that is located 120km (74mi) from their capital. And to protect the transportation of goods, they established secondary centers every 20km (12mi) along the route that connected Chichén Itzá to its port.

That ambitious project allowed this city to connect with many non-Maya cities through its trading alliances. Beside material gains, this allowed Chichén Itzá to culturally interact with other Mesoamerican civilizations. From that connection, the northern Maya incorporated some aspects of pan-Mesoamerican symbolism and motifs into their art. They combined it with artistic traditions, architecture, and rituals of the Classical period, which they also exported to other parts of Mesoamerica, mainly to their most important trade partners in central Mexico. From that mixture, a pan-Mesoamerican style evolved that was equally "global" as it was Maya. This cosmopolitan nature of Chichén Itzá certainly made trade and understanding with the foreigners easier, explaining how a city with a population of "only" 50 thousand managed to become a center of a trade network that covered almost entire Mesoamerica. But the change in art styles wasn't the most important change in Maya civilization at the time. The biggest shift was in the ruler's cult, which started to lose its strength. Slowly the scenes on the monuments started to depict groups of people in rituals and processions, instead of the portrayal of a single ruler that was common in the Classical era. New administrative buildings erected in this era could accommodate large groups of people, while the ball game courts became more important, also symbolizing the move to a more pluralistic society. With the culmination of those changes, around 950 C.E., came the end of the Terminal Classical period, and Middle Maya civilization, giving rise to the Postclassic era.

Temple of the Warriors at Chichén Itzá. Source: https://commons.wikimedia.org

Even though the ruler cult was getting weaker, and the economy and trade was the base of Chichén Itzá's power, the state also expanded through war and conquest of its weaker neighbors. Yet unlike the Classic period, those victories were secured by the new flexible political system that arose in the Postclassic era. Evident from the construction of council houses, called Popol Nah in Mayan, used for both commercial and political activities the ruling over the Chichén Itzá state was not solely in hands of the king. It is more likely he shared it with the council of the elite lords, both from the capital and to a certain extent other localities. And it seems that as time passed council's influence grew as the ruler's faded. Though it may seem counterintuitive that the decentralization of power would help the stability of the state, it actually was crucial. First of all, the new system disassociated the rulers of Chichén Itzá with the failed dynasties of the Classical era. Secondly, it lessened the political turmoil that usually came with changes on the throne, while at the same time lessened dependency of the state on the individual capabilities of the king. As the ruler shared the responsibility of decision making with the lords, their collective abilities could "fill in the gaps" that their leader may have. Finally, many of the lords and their families that came from the conquered cities, besides being political advisors, were effectively hostages, preventing their hometowns from revolting too often.

But the stability of the new system of rule wasn't enough to ensure Chichén Itzá's survival for long in the Postclassic era. In the mid-11th century C.E., power and influence of this state started to decline, and around 1100 C.E., it suffered destruction caused by war marking an end of the Chichén Itzá. The site wasn't completely abandoned, but any kind of political strength was gone. Historians today aren't exactly sure what caused the decline and fall of Chichén Itzá, as the evidence is scant. The military loss was only a part of it, as it was probably caused by an already weakened economy and lessened might of this city. Currently, the most likely theory is that the downfall was triggered by similar causes that led to the fall of Late Classic states, droughts, and the disruption of trade. And like before, it wasn't limited to just one or only a few of the cities, but it was an issue that impacted the entire Maya world as well as other parts of Mesoamerica. The disruption caused by these factors, unlike before, left the Maya civilization without a dominant power for about a century, indicating that the issues were too severe for the Maya to overcome as easily as when they were just exiting their golden age. By the time the new crisis hit the Maya, their might and wealth were considerably lower than in the Late Classic era. Yet this doesn't mean the Maya civilization completely collapsed: it was yet another hiatus.

When the hiatus ended around 1200 C.E., the Maya entered the Late Postclassic era that marked a complete shift from the hallmarks of the Middle Maya civilization. The most notable change was further development of Chichén Itzá's rule system that became known as "multepal;" roughly translated from Yucatec Mayan it means "joint rule." This type of government relied on various elites that weren't part of the royal family to fulfill more active and acknowledged roles in the state, while the ruler cult tradition was almost lost. That change was followed by decentralization of the state seen in the lack of large urban centers. Cities were considerably smaller but much better fortified. And in that period, they were usually built on hilltops instead of the valleys. Another change in society was that the Maya became more oriented towards entrepreneurship and profit instead of displays of royal power. Wealth was now much less invested in major public projects, and it seems that almost all citizens were directly or indirectly involved in the trade. With the much wider spread of profit gained through trade, the social distinction between classes became less prominent.

In the northern Lowlands, on the Yucatan peninsula, the best and probably the only example of this change is the city and state of Mayapan. The city was founded around 1185 C.E., roughly 100km (62mi) west of Chichén Itzá, whose architectural style it tried to mimic, but on a much smaller scale. Covering an area of only about 4.2km^2 (1.6mi^2) and with a population of 15 to 20 thousand, it was considerably smaller than its role model, not to mention that Late Classic centers were 10 to 12 times bigger than it. It clearly shows how drastically the power of the Maya states had decayed. But in contrast to its giant predecessors, Mayapan was much better fortified, with encircling walls and four gateways that were carefully planned to offer best possible protection from enemy attacks. The copying of Chichén Itzá, as well as some other former Maya powers, wasn't only smaller in scale, but buildings were erected with inferior craftsmanship, which also indicated the fall of the Maya civilization, especially considering the fact that the Mayapan was undoubtedly the wealthiest and most powerful city of the Late Postclassic period.

Mayapan's power came from the salt trade, similar to the Chichén Itzá, even though Mayapan was 40km (25mi) away from the coast. Another important resource was the rare clay which when mixed with indigo made the highly desired "Maya blue," which was even exported to the Aztecs in Central Mexico. But the connection with that part of Mesoamerica went beyond just trade. Many lord houses ruled Mayapan in a fully developed multepal system of government in which members of each house took part in both civil and religious offices. One of the houses known as the Cocom originated from Chichén Itzá and used mercenaries from the Aztec region to gain control over the city and the state from the original founder house of Xiu. That shift in the balance of the lord families happened in the last decades of the 13th century C.E. and could explain why later rulers of Mayapan tried to copy the style of Chichén Itzá. The Cocom house didn't stop there and, in a move to secure their supremacy in the state affairs, they expelled large part of the defeated Xiu family around 1400 C.E. That action is what eventually led to the fall of Mayapan state.

The territory of Mayapan was divided into provinces which were organized into a state that was more similar to a confederacy than a true monarchy. Centralization of the Mayapan state was secured with the fact that the leaders of each province actually lived in the capital, making it easier for the rulers to keep a close eye on them, and prevent them from rebelling. But when the Cocom exiled the Xiu instead of weakening them, they just left them largely uncontrolled. Bitter and driven by revenge members of the banished house organized a revolt in 1441 C.E. The city of Mayapan was sacked and destroyed, while almost all members of the Cocom dynasty were brutally killed. Soon afterward the city was abandoned and the last centralized state of the northern Maya had fallen. It territory fragmented into about 16 petty kingdoms, most likely corresponding to some extent to former provinces, ruled by other surviving elite houses. As the rivalry between them continued, they were locked in a cycle of constant infighting. By the mid-15th century C.E. all of the northern Maya economic might and political influence was gone, and the capitals of the petty kingdoms were only a pale comparison even to Mayapan, not to mention the cities of the golden age.

Panoramic view of Myapan. Source: https://commons.wikimedia.org

But unlike during the Classical era when the Lowlands was the only region that was influential, during the Late Postclassic Maya civilization the Highlands managed once again to grow strong enough to compete with their northern brethren. That power came from forming of Quiché (or alternatively known as K'iche) Confederacy, which first became an important factor in late 14th and early 15th century under the rule of king K'ucumatz ("Feathered Serpent") who managed to grasp control of central Guatemalan highlands through series of wars and conquests. His successors continued to expand their kingdom, which spanned from present-day El Salvador to southeastern Mexico, including the Pacific Coast region, which by that time had managed to recover from the volcanic eruption that ended the Preclassic period. It was one of the biggest Maya states in history covering an area of about 67.500km^2 (26.000mi^2) with an estimated population of around one million Maya. That massive kingdom was, like Mayapan, governed by the multepal system, which was one of the reasons why it managed to grow exponentially. But it was probably also the reason why the Quiché state broke up rather quickly, by the end of the 15th-century C.E.

The cause of fragmentation of the Quiché kingdom was a rebellion of one of the elite houses in the state around 1475 C.E. The success of that revolt sparked other allies and lords to rise up as well, and by the beginning of the 16th century, the Highlands were no longer united. By the time the Spaniards came, the Quiché were no longer at their peak, but the Europeans were impressed by the capital of Utatlán. It was a somewhat small urban center located in one of the hilltops of the Guatemalan highlands with a population of about 15 thousand. The heavy fortification of the city, which to a degree resembled the citadels of medieval Europe, was the thing that impressed the Conquistadors the most. From their records, it is clear the Spaniards saw the Quiché capital as a threat because of the fortification, that the only choice they had was to destroy it, which they eventually did. Yet, no matter how impressive the Utatlán stronghold was, for historians today the more important aspect of this settlement was its role in culture and civilization of the Maya, as well as our present understanding of their civilization.

One of the characteristics of the Quiché was that they acted as a cultural center of the Late Postclassic period of the Maya civilization. Their capital, city of Utatlán, was also the main hub for learning, writing religious books, and histories marked with so-called Maya calendar dates. One of those books is the famous Popol Vuh, which is one of the main sources on Maya mythology today. It was written down in the mid-16th century, but it was based on a long oral tradition of the Maya. Unfortunately, other books of the Quiché were mostly destroyed by the Spaniards who saw them as satanic due to the hieroglyphic writing in them. Besides the written records, the cultural strength and development of Utatlán are clearly shown in public works which weren't something that could be commonly seen in the northern Maya cities. The site contains four impressively-decorated temples, a ball court, and even a small pyramid only 18m (60ft) high. One of the more interesting details of these buildings detected by historians today are the clear signs of influence from the Central Mexican art style and the Aztec civilization.

Considering that by the late 15th and early 16th century C.E. the Aztecs were the most powerful and influential nation in Mesoamerica, the Aztec influence on Maya style shouldn't be much of a surprise. Especially considering how weak the Maya civilization had become by that period. Their art style, fashion, and architecture influenced all the Maya, from the Pacific Coast to the Lowlands. They used Aztec style to depict their own traditional Maya themes, while some cities even tried to mimic the architectural features of the Aztec capital. But their influence went even further than that. The Aztec supremacy in both cultural and economic power made Nahuatl, the Aztec language, the lingua franca of the Mesoamerican region. It was surely the main language spoken among the traders and in ports, as witnessed by the Spaniards. But some of the Maya nobles learned Nahuatl, both for prestige but also for use in diplomacy. In certain areas, the Aztec empire wasn't content with simply trading with the locals. For example, in 1500 C.E., they exploited the turmoil in the Quiché kingdom and attacked the cacao-rich western borders. The result of those attacks was the tribute the Quiché started to pay to the mighty Aztec empire. It seems they were also preparing to do something similar on Yucatan as well, but the arrival of Spaniards foiled their plans.

It wasn't long before the Aztecs realized that the Europeans posed a serious threat for entire Mesoamerica, and their famous emperor Montezuma (or Moctezuma) urged the Maya to unite against new conquerors from across the ocean. It seems that the Quiché were ready to follow that advice, but before any definitive steps could be taken the Aztec empire had fallen. With the only political power capable to unite the fragmented Maya states against the Spaniards gone, any chance of united front was gone. The first region that became targeted by Europeans was the Highlands in 1524 C.E.

Despite the pleas of the Quiché to other states of the region to unite their forces against the Conquistadors; other Maya states were more interested in defeating traditional enemies that fighting against a new threat. With the help of the local Maya, the Quiché state quickly fell. Soon the other Maya states realized that both the Aztecs and the Quiché were right, Spaniards were the biggest threat to them all. But it was too late and by 1530 C.E., the Highlands and the Pacific Coast were under the Spanish flag.

It is unclear if the Yucatan Maya learned from the mistakes of their Highland brethren, or if it was just common sense, but when the Conquistadors first arrived on their territory in 1527 C.E., they fought more coordinated and united against the invaders, pushing them back despite losing a few battles. The Spaniards came back in 1530, but after initial success, the Maya were again able to organize a unified front against them and in 1535 C.E., Yucatan was once again free of the Europeans. Unfortunately for the Maya, when the Spaniards came back in 1541 C.E., their two biggest royal families, the Xiu and Cocom, were once again at war with each other. Without the ability to act together one more time to thwart yet another invasion of Conquistadors, the Maya were quickly defeated. The last organized attempt of resistance happened in 1546 when the majority of the Yucatan Maya revolted, but in the end, their resistance was futile. The Spaniards almost completely conquered the Maya homeland. Some of the Maya stated to flee from their cities to the more remote areas, creating small enclaves where they continued to live in the traditional way. But even those fell under the colonial rule one by one. With the fall of Tah Itzá (Tayasal), a city located in Northern Guatemala, in 1697 C.E., pre-Columbian Maya civilization was finally brought to an end.

The Spanish conquest of the Maya region was in every way a disastrous event for the Maya. The most tragic outcome of this event was the death of up to 90% of the entire Maya population. This was caused in part by war and enslavement, but most of the Maya fell as victims of diseases brought by Europeans. Historians today see those as one of the major reasons for such an easy defeat of both the Maya and the Aztecs, as illnesses weakened the Mesoamericans. Yet the disaster for the Maya didn't end there. Spanish Catholic missionaries saw the Maya culture and religion as heathen and evil, so they aimed to "save" them by forcing them to convert, burning their books and smashing their monuments. The severe consequences of these actions led to massive cultural dislocation even led to some of the Maya refusing to have children. This brutal, almost apocalyptic end of the Maya civilization caused it to be lost and forgotten for a long time, but in spite of this, the Maya have endured to this day.

Chapter 5 – The Maya government and society

As it was shown in previous chapters, the Maya were never able to unite their entire ethnos into a single unified empire, remaining spread into many larger and smaller states. Yet through ideology and beliefs, religion, and culture, they remained a relatively homogenous group. The closest comparison from the "old world" would be ancient Greeks, who suffered a similar fate. Despite that, the Maya for a long time suffered from closemindedness and prejudice on the part of historians who simply could not believe that "savages," as the Conquistadors saw the Maya, could have created a civilization that could rival, or even be compared to, the "forefathers of the western civilization."   For that reason, during much of the 20th-century historians believed that the Maya never even managed to form more complex governments. The dominant theory of that time was that the Maya world remained divided into small chiefdoms, with a simple two-class society. But as the more evidence was gathered, historians realized they were wrong

As the archeologists surveyed more Maya sites they found the public projects, from irrigation canals to grand palaces. Then the more detailed mapping of some larger sites showed the researchers that the site was more densely populated. Finally, when the Maya text was deciphered, showing complex hierarchy between the cities, it became clear beyond a doubt that by the end of the Late Preclassic period the Maya society and politics became so complex that they had developed into preindustrial states. That same evidence also debunked yet another misconception about the Maya sites, which were for a long time seen only as ceremonial and market centers of chiefdoms. Archeologists concluded this as they only understood dates and astronomical information which could be read from the inscriptions, and also because the street grid and population density were not as high as in industrial era cities of Europe. But when they took their focus away from large and mainly intact temples, they found remains of many smaller buildings covered by vegetation. After careful examination, it became clear that more than 80% of those were, in fact, residential buildings. That combined with deciphered texts showing of all the complexity of Maya history made the theory of the ceremonial center discredited. The Maya settlements were in fact cities, in a true sense of the word, with at least 20 of them having a population greater than 50 thousand during the golden age of the Classic era.

But even before the glory days of the late classic period, during the last centuries of the Preclassic era, the Maya managed to evolve from simple chiefdoms into states. The main characteristic of chiefdoms was a simpler division of the population into two classes; elites, and commoners, with a shaman-ruler above all others. Yet as their power expanded, so did the area the chiefdoms ruled, creating a three-tier hierarchy of settlements in those larger polities. With that, the Maya society slowly started to create a new middle class. That combined with the increasing strength of the ruler cult was enough for historians to claim that the Maya polities of the Late Preclassic have evolved into early, archaic states. The rise of the Maya society complexity continued in later periods, reaching its limits in the Late Classic era where states managed to develop a five-tier hierarchy of the settlements. On top was, of course, the capital, followed by secondary centers, then came smaller towns, and final to tiers were villages and hamlets. And some of those smaller sites started to specialize in certain fields like trade, stone quarrying or artisanry.

Both of those echoed in the social structure of the Maya society, which by that time had stratified both vertically and horizontally.

Painting of a Maya scribe. Source: https://commons.wikimedia.org

On top of that social structure was undoubtedly the king, but the topic of the ruler cult will come later in this chapter, as it is a complex topic that deserves a lot more than just a few sentences. Below the monarch were the elite, which represented about one-tenth of the entire population. Position in this class was represented by both wealth and lineage, and it wasn't easy for non-nobles to move up the social ladder into this caste. The nobles were sometimes called "itz'at winik," which roughly translates to "wise people," which probably referred to their better education and literacy. Most of this class held important positions in the society as higher priests, overseers of the secondary centers, scribes, and in some cases even artists. Below, the elite was the middle class, which wasn't a tight homogenous group as previously thought. This class had various levels of social importance and wealth. It was constituted of low-level priests and government officials, professional soldiers, merchant, and artisans. But it is rather important to note that the line between these two classes is often blurred. Some of the elites were also merchants and warriors, while in some cases middle-class members managed to become high-level officers. And in some cases, certain members of the middle class were as wealthy as the elite, while there were also examples of impoverished elite members. More than occupation and wealth, the main difference between these classes seems to be family and lineage of the individual, which was important to the Maya.

Below these two subsets were commoners, who unlike two other classes were rarely shown in art and never mentioned in texts. Yet they were the enormous majority which was the base of the entire Maya society. Most of them were farmers, laborers, unskilled craftsmen, and servants. They lived in villages and outskirts of cities, in relative poverty when compared to the higher classes. But when archeologists excavated a village that was covered by a volcanic eruption around 600 C.E., they found out that even the commoners had decent lives. Researchers even noted that living conditions there were even better than those of the 20th-century Salvadoran workers who helped in the excavation of the site. Farmers, which were the backbone of the society, usually worked on their own or their family land, but a number of the landless farmers worked on estates of the nobles, which were inherited with the land. The lowest class of the Maya society were slaves, which actually weren't that numerous. Most of them were commoners captured in war, as the captured nobles were often sacrificed, and the elite used them as a labor force. In some cases, thieves were also enslaved so they could repay what they stole. Interestingly, unlike most other societies in the world, the Maya didn't consider children of the slaves to be slaves as well. Those children were given the chance to live their lives according to their abilities and weren't made to pay the price of their parents "mistakes."

Social structure started to change with the transition from the Late Classic to the Postclassic Maya civilization. With the development of multepal system rulers started to lose power, and nobles were even able in some cases to rival the royal dynasty. The flattening of the vertical social hierarchy went further down, as the goods that were previously available only to the elite class, like shells, obsidian, and ceramics became more widely distributed and attainable even for commoners. Distinction and difference in wealth between these classes were lessened; in some cases, it could be even claimed the middle class had disappeared. This could have happened if the only division between the elite and non-elite was the lineage and knowledge about the religious rituals. But at the same time, it would seem that the horizontal social structure grew. With the rise of multepal system, bureaucratic apparatus grew both in size and complexity, making government officials more numerous than ever before, with more intricate hierarchical ranks. Of course, higher and more important ranks were reserved for members of the elite, and were usually hereditary, while the lower ranks were open to commoners who were appointed only for a period of time.

After it became abundantly clear that the Maya had developed states and that their society was more intricate than was thought before, the next issue of debate between historians was about the nature of those states. One theory is that the Maya polities were, in fact, city-states that only controlled their nearest surrounding areas, up to 20km (12.5 mi) around them. That is based on an approximation of the how far could the Maya travel in one day by foot, limiting the efficient communication, transport, and control of the capital. And according to this theory, no matter how sizeable the capital was, it wouldn't be able to sufficiently rule over area further than that. Contrary to this, there is a theory of the so-called regional state, arguing that the Maya capitals managed to extend their limit of control via secondary centers, which would be close enough to be controlled from the capital. Thus, the secondary centers would in turn extend the reach of the capital by at least another 20km (12.5 mi), or even more if we add to that a secondary center, which would further expand that control to another secondary or tertiary city. This theory fits amazingly well with the distance between secondary centers of Chichén Itzá that guarded the path to its port. Yet when all is considered, both theories aren't exactly in agreement with the current archeological findings.

Furthering the problem is the fact that those two theories are polar opposites. The best illustration of the differences between those two ideas is the issue of Late Classic states, around 790 C.E. 60 sites met the criteria of city-state theory. If the regional states theory is applied, however, there were only eight. The problem is that evidence shows there were significant connections and interaction between the states, supporting the regional state model. But at the same time, warfare, political instability, and clashes between the cities that were supposedly controlled by one of the capitals support the concept of a city-state. So, in an attempt to somehow bridge the gap between two opposing theories, historians created the so-called "superstates" theory. According to this theory, in certain cases, the power of a single Maya state grew so much that it managed to create dominance over a large territory, but instead of ruling it directly, those political formations were more of a vassal confederacy in which smaller autonomous states paid tributes to the capital.

Military conquest or simple threat didn't in all cases force these autonomous vassalages. In some cases, smaller states simply gained prestige by allying to the major power. So, they willingly became part of these superstates. Dynastic marriages and trade networks sometimes reinforced the connections between the states. Of course, in some cases, superpowers conquered weaker states and installed rulers loyal to them. And these confederacy superstates existed as long as the central states were powerful enough to maintain them. At the first sign of weakness, they would start to crumble. But also, as soon as the central states' power was reestablished, the superstate would build up quickly. This theory is still being developed, yet it seems to be the best explanation of the Late Classic politics of Tikal and Calakmul. It can reconcile the fact that influence and control of those Classic Maya superpowers was wide-reaching, while at the same time the Maya homeland seemed to be covered with independent city-states. Another plus for this theory is that it seems to be more of a typical Mesoamerican type of rule since it also resembles the way the Aztec empire functioned. And the only reason why historians haven't yet elevated Calakmul and Tikal to the rank of empires is the fact that their reach never extended outside the Maya region.

Despite the uncertainty about the size and exact nature of the Maya states, historians are sure of one thing. Monarchs ruled the Maya states. That has been the case since the early ages of the Maya civilization when first individual rulers became powerful enough to leave behind monuments and inscriptions. In those early times, those monarchs used the title "ajaw," which we today translate as either king or lord. During the Middle Maya civilization, to emphasize their even greater strength and position in the social hierarchy of the society, Maya rulers started calling themselves "k'uhul ajaw," which is roughly equivalent to as divine or holy lord/king. For some rulers of Tikal that alone wasn't enough, so they also used "kaloomte'", a title that is today translated as supreme king, but this title wasn't as widespread. Interestingly, the rulers who were subjugated to their more powerful neighbors still used the same title, k'uhul ajaw, but they also added they were "yajaw," or vassal lord, of some other king. But no matter what title a ruler used, one thing remained the same through the almost entire history of the Maya civilization. The base of the monarch's control of the subordinated population was rooted in his economic supremacy and religious importance.

Stelae of the 13th Ajaw of the Copán Dynasty. Source:
https://commons.wikimedia.org

The religious authority of the Maya rulers has its root in the era of chiefdoms, where chiefs were also shamans, able to communicate with deified ancestors and mediate with the gods. But when the society grew more complex, and the power of the rulers increased, kings started to claim they were direct descendants of the gods, similar to the pharaohs of ancient Egypt. Thus, the rulers' cult was created, in which kings themselves were revered as divine. This was evident from the title of k'uhul ajaw. With religious authority behind them, they became important for carrying out certain religious rituals and ceremonies done for the benefit of the entire state. But theocratic power alone wasn't enough to cement their supremacy in the society. Royal dynasties were also the wealthiest, and their power was based on control of important resources. Sometimes it was water or food, in other cases maybe obsidian or other valuable export goods. Through the control of those resources, rulers gained enough wealth to reward those who were obedient and also to pay for great public works and other exhibitions of power and prosperity. But at the same time, rulers threw state feasts through which they demonstrated their ability to provide for the entire population, not only the Royals. Of course, that kind of spending together with economic supremacy was more easily maintained since almost the entire population, with the possible exception of the highest nobility and members of the royal family, paid tributes to the ruler. Though economic and religious authority created a strong base for absolute rule, it was also a double-edged sword.

If the ruler was capable and had a bit of luck on his side, his authority was unquestionable. But if he lost a battle, if trade routes were cut or even if the harvest wasn't good enough, it was seen as a bad omen. It meant the king had lost the favor of the gods. Both his religious and economic supremacy were shaken. Those kinds of disasters could topple dynasties and crush entire states. When we consider that fact, it becomes clearer why after a single defeat or other sign of weakness many vassals decided to either switch sides or simply declare independence. That is why the Maya often tried to capture and sacrifice the enemy's king. It was the ultimate sign of weakness, which in some cases dealt such a religious and political blow to a state that it could never fully recover. On the other hand, long and successful rules like the one of Yuknoom the Great, meant the king was in the good graces of the gods, attracting more and more allies as time passed. When all that is taken into account, it seems that the authority of the Maya rulers relied only upon individual charisma and capabilities. A ruler had to be a victorious general, successful diplomat, and a fortunate religious leader. But as we have seen, the Maya cared a lot about family and lineage. This was even more important for the ajaws and their dynastic ties.

Dynasties in the Maya world, especially during the Classic period, were extremely important, as they were probably the most important thing that connected the ruler to his divinity. Without a connection to a deified ancestor, kings wouldn't be holy. That is one of the reasons why the Maya kept such close records of their rulers, and always held the founding ruler of the city in special regard. This connection gave legitimacy to the successors. Another dimension to the importance of dynasties in the Maya society comes from their tradition of worshiping their ancestors. And the royal families represented the most powerful and most important ancestors. Going against their heirs might upset the powerful forefathers. Dynastic ties weren't only achievable by birth, however. They were also created through marriage, similar to medieval Europe. A smaller state and dynasty would gain in prestige if a king's bride came from a strong and respected lineage. This helped not only in foreign affairs, but also to strengthen the authority of the ruler in his own state. A good example of that is the already mentioned marriage between a Naranjo noble and Dos Pilas princess. Her bloodline elevated this noble, and their heirs, to a royal family.

Although this shows to a degree how important woman could get into Maya politics, it wasn't their only means of power. The Maya dynasties were patrilineal, but in certain extreme cases when the male line, from father to son, was broken they could become matrilineal as well. That way the state was preserving the royal family and connection to the founding king through the blood of the queen or a princess, which would in that instance become the ruler. So far historians have found only five examples of this, though there could be more. Among the examples we see two different examples of women rulers. One was the example when they briefly ruled as regents to their sons, which was something that was common in dynasties around the world. One of those was the previously mentioned princess that went to Naranjo, Lady Wac-Chanil-Ahau, also known as Lady Six Sky. Although she was probably never crowned, she unquestionably ruled over that city during the end of 7th and at the beginning of the 8th century C.E. Lady Six Sky took on religious roles, got involved in diplomacy, with some monuments even depicting her in warrior-king form, probably due the fact that Naranjo achieved some rather impressive military victors under her rule. But one of the queens, Yohl Ik'nal of Palenque, actually ruled with full titles of the king, as if she was a male heir of the dynasty. Lady Heart of the Wind Place, as she was known, ruled from 583 to 604 C.E. Not much is known about her reign, but she kept the direct blood connection of the future rulers with the founder of the Palenque, as the same royal family stayed in power. This was an important flexibility that provided an extra level of stability on the throne of the Maya states.

Yet no matter how flexible the Maya dynasties were, none of them were really eternal. Some of them died out naturally, other violently. Some were dethroned by outsiders, others by their own nobles. It would then be reasonable to assume with an end of one dynasty, the link with the founding king and the ancestor would be broken, especially if the new monarch came from outside of the community, placed on the throne by a king of another state. But that wasn't the case. All rulers of a single city claimed they were continuing the line from the scared founder. That kind of regal continuum is clearly marked by the fact that the Maya numbered their rulers, starting from the founder. A great example of this is the takeover of Tikal in 378 C.E. When Yax Nuun Ayiin was crowned as a king, he was marked as the fifteenth successor to Yax Ehb Xook, the founder of the city. And he wasn't even trying to present himself as a legitimate pretender for the throne. In that way, the title of k'uhul ajaw could on its own give authority and power to the bearer and his successors, as its connection to the founding father was more symbolic than realistic.

What was certainly real was the power of the king, which at the height of the rulers' cult, was unquestionable. But even the mightiest and most capable monarch couldn't rule the whole state on his own, especially ones as big as Tikal and Calakmul. That is why it comes as no surprise that nobles served the ruler in his higher-ranking administrative offices. Even the title, "sajal," that was awarded to king's official hints at it, as the literal translation is "noble." There was also a position of "baah sajal," or head noble, which probably was in charge of several sajals, reporting directly to the king himself. Of course, there were more titles reserved for the elite, like "ah tz'ihb" or royal scribe. And exact roles in a court of some titles, like "yajaw k'ahk'", or lord of fire, still remain a mystery for the historians. Nonetheless, it clearly shows that the Maya rulers had to rely on the help of their elite to effectively rule their growing states. At the same time, it was another way of binding the nobles to their rule, as those titles were also given to governors of secondary and tertiary sites.

This kind of "buying" and confirming the loyalty of the elite worked as long as the kings were successful. But this political maneuver backfired for the later rulers in the Terminal Classic and Postclassic era, when the royal cult started to die off. Powers given to the nobles became too much to control, and the elite were unhappy with the end result of the monarchs' rule. They eventually started to limit the authority of their rulers. An example of this is seen through the creation of the council house, the Popol Nah. No longer could the Maya kings rule absolutely; they had the noble council to answer to. At the same time, nobles were able to advise their ruler more and steer the state politics more to their liking. An example of this council type of monarchy is seen in 9th century Copan, where archeologists found a Popol Nah decorated with glyphs representing various noble lineages, proving that this building wasn't created solely for the ruler and the royal family. Today historians assume that during the Terminal Classic period there was tension between the royal and noble families, if not more open struggle for powers. But the lack of evidence prevents them from creating a more accurate picture of that.

What is certainly clearer is the fact that, as the ruler cult was more frequently abandoned in the Late Postclassic era, the council system evolved into the multepal system. In theory, it was a system of joint rule by several noble houses, which didn't necessarily need to originate from the state capital. But this oligarchy system actually rarely worked as intended. The flaws are best seen in the example of Mayapan. This state was certainly formed with the multepal system, in which several noble houses ruled together, sharing government offices among them. But after a short time, it became clear that one house, the Cocom, had become stronger than others, since its leader assumed the role of the king. He even kept representatives of other noble families as hostages in the capital. Although his rule wasn't as absolute as the rule of Late Classic kings, it wasn't a true multepal anymore. But the Maya didn't completely abandon the idea of the joint rule. After the Mayapan state collapsed, many smaller states were created. Most of them were ruled by kings, now holding the title of "halach uinic," meaning real/true man, supported by influential councils. The title itself is one more proof of the failing rulers' cult. But more fascinating are several smaller states whose texts don't mention halach uinic at all, only councils. These seem to be an example of a real and functional multepal system. Sadly, any further development of this system and the idea of the shared rule in the Maya civilization was abruptly halted by the conquest of the Spaniards.

So far, the topic of the governmental rule was only examined looking at the highest levels of the state, rulers and noble councils, and focused primarily on the capital. Of course, this is rather reasonable considering these were the most important factors in the government, but also because other lower ranks of the government system weren't mentioned in the Maya texts. This lack of evidence was somewhat lessened with the archeological evidence found at Cerén, a classic period site in western El Salvador. Around 600 C.E., this small village, with a population of about 200 people, was covered by ash during a volcanic eruption. Archeologists have found that the largest building of the site, with the thickest walls, lacked any common household items, but it was fitted with two benches on the sidewalls and a large jar near one of them. The interior walls also have signs of decoration in the form of lines and punctuation. All this led the researchers to conclude that this was a public building, most likely used for local governance and community meetings. Village elders and leaders would gather on the benches, discuss local affairs, make decisions, and settle any disputes in their community. Drink ladled from the large jar was probably used for the ceremonial purpose of sealing the actions of the community council. Furthermore, archeologists think that this "village hall" was used to deliberate on and announce any orders that came from the capital, as well to inform the villagers about their corvée labor duties. Even though most of these are assumptions made by archeologists based on scarce evidence, thanks to the "Pompeii of the Americas," we have at least a vague idea of how the Maya government system functioned on a local level.

Chapter 6 – The Maya warfare

It is evident both from Maya texts and monuments, as well as some other archeological findings, that warfare played an important role in Maya civilization. During most of their history, the fragmented Maya states were locked in the almost perpetual state of war among themselves. Not even the foreign threats, like ones coming from Teotihuacan or the Aztecs, could make the Maya call a truce and unite against the common enemy. When the Spaniards came, the Yucatan Maya recognized how dangerous the Europeans were, but even then, the urge to settle old scores was too great for peace and unity to last longer than a couple of years. It would be expected that something as crucial to the Maya as war would be well-documented, and fully understood by the historians, but that is not the case. Not much is known about logistics, the organization of the military, or their training, as they are not described or even mentioned in texts and carvings. Monuments sometimes contain depictions of battles, but mostly they focus on celebrating victories and mentioning wars waged by the Maya kings. This lack of concrete evidence hasn't discouraged archeologists and historians in their attempts to uncover at least some mysteries of Maya warfare.

One of the certainties of Maya warfare is that the rulers were supreme war captains, as evident from the monuments. In the Preclassic period rulers were depicted, and in some cases even buried, with trophy heads on their belts. Those represented the sacrificed captives. That imagery later disappeared, and rulers were represented standing on their captives. Sometimes even queens would be shown in the same way. Prisoners of war were important to the Maya kings, as it was a way of proving one's worth to both the gods and subordinates. Some documents testify that before a ruler could be crowned he had to capture at least one prisoner for sacrifice. In some scenes, even the royal ancestors, dressed as warriors, are depicted advising the current ruler on the battlefield. The religious importance of sacrifices, especially of the captives, persisted until the time of the Conquistadors, giving one explanation why warfare was important to the Maya and their kings. It also helps illustrate why wars apparently never stopped in the Maya world, and why rulers often took titles like "He of 20 Captives." Despite all the carvings and texts representing victorious rulers, some historians claimed that the Maya rulers weren't really participating in battles; that they were simply commanders-in-chief, not soldiers. They saw depictions as pure propaganda. Disregarding scenes of kings involved in hand-to-hand combat, the fact that many inscriptions mention rulers that were captured in battles and sacrificed later disproves this theory. Even the Spaniards mention that some of the royal families' heads fought against them in direct combat.

It was also the European conquerors who noted some of the organization and hierarchy of the Late Postclassic Maya military. Spaniards mention a nonhereditary military title of "nacom." This rank was not permanent, but held for a short period of time, not longer than the duration of a particular war, similar to the title of the dictator in the ancient Roman republic. Their task was to gather and organize the army, while also performing certain religious rituals that were likely formerly done by the ruler himself. A nacom from the Yucatan did not personally lead the troops into the fight, but only acted as a chief military strategist. But in the Quiché kingdom, nacom also led the troops in battle, supported by four captains under his command. Those captains were likely ranked as "batab," a title that was given to the rulers and governors of dependent towns and sites within the state. The Spaniards recorded that their obligation was to lead their local armies into the battle under the supreme command of their ruler, or in this case an officer representing the ruler. Historians have linked the responsibilities and duties to the Late Classical period title of sahal, also given to the rulers of vassal cities.

Another Classical period military rank that has been deciphered is the title of "bate." Its true nature remains hidden, but it seems it has something to do with war captives and their sacrifice. This title has been held by both the ruler and the elite warriors, but it's been also attributed to some noblewomen. Although there are some mentions of women assisting in war, they were never mentioned as military officers. So, it seems that bate was a more honorific and hereditary title, given to a person or a family that demonstrated worth in combat. The thing that connects all known military officers is that they were all restricted to the members of the elite, whether they were hereditary or not. This was probably due to the fact that only nobles had any possibility to practice the art of war and of strategy. But having nobles serve as military officers was also beneficial to the ruler and the state as they could raise a large number of warriors through their kinship, tribute relations, and direct control of their lands. This can be compared to feudal lords in European medieval kingdoms. A major difference between the Maya noble officers and the European knights is that in the Maya society a commoner could advance through both military and social ranks if he could prove his prowess in warfare.

Historians today can't be sure how common that type of the advancement was, but it is clear that below the officers came the majority of commoner soldiers. The Maya didn't have a standing army, but some sources suggest they had a small group of warriors stationed in larger settlements, always prepared for battle. Whether these were commoners or members of the elite is uncertain. Whatever was the case, Spaniards report that every attempted surprise attack on the ports was met by a group of the Maya prepared to fight. The regular Maya soldiers were actually conscripts, most likely gathered by their local governors or lords. Their military service may also have been part of corvée labor duties. Service of the common folk was especially needed in times of the full-scale wars, when the majority of the adult male population was conscripted to fight for their king and their state. It is likely they brought their own weapons, used in the peacetime for hunting. And it seems that hunting was the only training a commoner got, which was later expanded by his own experience from previous military campaigns he was involved in. During periods of war, another type of soldiers used were mercenaries. Better trained, yet less loyal, they were in some cases a decisive factor in the course of the war. Their payments were given to them by the war captains who bought their services, but the common citizens housed and fed them.

Mercenaries, as well as the officers and common recruits, brought their own weapons on the battlefield. The most commonly depicted weapon on the monuments is probably the "atlatl" or the spear-thrower. This weapon was brought to the Maya world from Central Mexico by Teotihuacanos around the 4th century C.E. It was a major improvement as the javelin or a dart, with its sharpened chert or obsidian tip, could hit a target from a distance of 45m (150 ft), with at least twice as much force and better accuracy than if it was done by simply throwing. It should be noted that some historians think the use of the atlatl was limited, due to its impracticality in the jungle terrain, claiming that its depictions were common only as a symbol of power borrowed from Teotihuacan art. Beside the spear-thrower, the Maya also used blowguns, which were used in both hunting and in war. This weapon was more likely used by the commoners, as it was cheaper to make, and required less training. Bow and arrow were also known as far back as the Classical era, but it was not until the Postclassic times that it became a common weapon on the battlefield. It was also more commonly associated with the non-elite soldiers, who used reed arrows, pointed with flints or sharp fish teeth. Beside those, the Maya used a variety of hand-to-hand weapons.

The Maya soldiers commonly used wooden spears, axes, and clubs, which were all commonly fitted with razor-sharp obsidian spikes or blades. They had knives and daggers, also made from sharpened obsidian or flint. For Europeans the lack of metal weapons was strange, and they considered it rather primitive. But the Maya by the time of the arrival of first Spaniards already used copper blades, albeit on a limited scale. In general, they tended to stick with stone cutting edges since obsidian was more common, cheaper, more durable, and easier to convert into sharp blades. Also, there was nothing primitive about the obsidian blade, for Christopher Columbus himself noted that the Maya weapons cut as well as the Spanish steel. The Maya warriors were often further equipped with shields. The type of shield used depended mainly on the weapon a soldier was carrying. If armed with a spear, a Maya fighter would usually carry a rectangular flexible shield made out of leather and cotton. Their defensive capabilities were limited and these shields were mostly used to protect from projectiles and give more passive protection to the body. It was most likely that the spear provided both attacking strikes and active defensive parrying. And historians think these spearmen were the most common type of Maya warriors utilized in battles, making them the core of the army.

Ax or club-wielding soldiers were less common and were most likely used to complement the spearmen in battle, or perhaps they were given more specialized tasks. They were also more valuable in small raids on lightly-armored enemies. These types of warriors also carried shields. Usually, those were round and more rigid, made out of leather, wood, and in some cases even tortoise shells. As they were smaller and tightly strapped to the arm, their main use was in parrying the blows of the enemy, as the shorter clubs and axes weren't adequate for that purpose. This type of shield eschewed a larger, more protective size in favor of a smaller, but more maneuverable form. This to a degree lessened the amount of protection the shield provided a warrior. Archeologists have also found a third type of shield which was a rigid, large, and rectangular;

it was usually made out of wood, leather, or woven reeds. This was a Central Mexican introduction, as it was more common in that area. But historians assume its use was limited, mostly intended as a sign of power and prestige. This theory comes from the shield's impracticality in the thick jungles of the Maya homeland, and also from the fact that the shields were commonly associated with the Mexican-style iconography and gods, giving the shield more value as a status symbol.

A figurine of the Maya spearman. Source: https://commons.wikimedia.org

It seems that helmets were also somewhat symbolic. They were usually worn by higher-ranking officers, and although they probably offered some added protection, their main use was to represent the status of the wearer. In the Postclassic era, those helmets, usually made out of wood, were adorned with various emblems, effigies, and feathers. Ones from the classical period were even less protective, and more aesthetic. Those were more elaborate wooden and cloth headdresses that most likely represented the spirit animal of the warrior. Carrying the symbolism even further were the kings. In some cases, the Maya rulers would dress in ritual war costumes to inspire their troops. This clothing would offer some extra protection but would be too impractical for combat. That is why it wasn't a common practice and was most likely used in cases when the king wasn't directly involved in the actual fighting. In more usual depictions of rulers in battle, they wore more suitable clothing for protection, like quilted cotton vests and jaguar-pelt leggings. They also carried elaborate jaguar headdresses and shields adorned with the symbol of the jaguar sun god, a Maya deity of war and the Underworld.

Despite the fact the kings were sometimes depicted wearing quilted cotton armor, its usage doesn't seem to have been that common. Most of the common warriors are depicted wearing nothing but a loincloth. So, it seems that, at least in the Classical era, cotton armor was reserved for the nobles. This may have changed in the Postclassic era, as there are records that the Spaniards have been dropping their own steel plates to switch to the Maya cotton tunics. This may indicate that more than just a few noblemen wore it. But it also proves how effective it was. It provided more than sufficient protection against obsidian-based arms, though Conquistador sources indicate that it was just a little bit less efficient against steel weapons. But its major advantages were that it was lighter, more suitable for the high temperatures of the region, and that it was more flexible, making soldiers more mobile than if they were wearing steel armor. Alas, that type of protection wasn't available to the commoners. Since they fought bare-chested, they often applied body paint on themselves. Reasons for that can be found in possible religious ceremonies, to differentiate themselves from the enemy, or even as a psychological warfare tactic to frighten the opponents.

The exact tactics used by the Maya generals on the battlefields are unknown to us as there are no records about them. Some historians argue that the lack of banners and standards points to the fact that they fought out of formation. Supporting evidence for this theory is the fact that dense jungles are not suitable terrain for armies to maintain order. What military historians assume, according to the types of weapons and equipment used by the Maya, is that typical battles started with volleys from projectile weapons. These were aimed at weakening the enemy, both physically and mentally. Then the main combatants of the armies would collide in hand-to-hand combat in a simple straightforward clash. Winners of these battles would be the ones with bigger armies, better equipment, and ultimately higher morale and will to fight. Of course, this can't discount the possibility that at least some Maya strategists used more complex tactics, like encirclement or ambushes. Historians simply don't have the evidence to confirm that possibility.

Not all Maya battles were in the wilderness, since an important tactic of Maya warfare was carrying out city raids. In some situations, the cities that were attacked were defenseless. For example, a defending city's main army might have been defeated prior to the urban attack. The attacking army could then just plow through the city, burning, pillaging, and causing destruction. But the cities weren't always left without any protection. In those cases, the broad streets and open plazas most likely turned into a fractioned battlefield. Of course, the fate of the city and its citizens depended on the result of the battle. As these attacks on the urban centers became more frequent, defenders started building various defensive structures which altered the way those cities were attacked. There is no evidence of siege equipment needed to break through the defenses, so it seems the main tactic was a blockade. The attacking army would try to cut off the city's supplies in hope that the defenders would eventually yield. Proficiency of the Maya in the use of this tactic was confirmed by the Spaniards, who were actually defeated by it during their attack on Yucatan in 1533 C.E. Their camp was surrounded, cut off from supplies. Unable to find food or water they were forced to run away during the night in an attempt to save their lives. Other possible siege tactics may have been used, like surprise attacks, catching the defensive forces off guard. Perhaps people in settlements may have been bribed to allow attacking armies entrance. Yet again, these tactics can't be concretely verified by the sources, so they remain the object of speculation.

Replica of a Maya mural depicting a battle. Source: https://commons.wikimedia.org

What is clearly evident are the remains of the fortifications used to defend cities from the attacks. It seems that initially the most common types of defense were ditches and moats created by diverting the agricultural canals. Some historians argue that moats weren't mainly defensive but were only used as water reservoirs for the city. Both theories about the use of moats are plausible. In peacetime people could use them as a water source. But, during an attack, moats would present a major obstacle to invading forces. Walls were also built, and some were up to 11m (36ft) high. There are fewer doubts about their purpose, as they are clearly made to be part of fortifications. Some have argued that the walls were erected to separate the nobility from the commoners, but it doesn't seem likely as it goes against the Maya idea of open public spaces for rituals and ceremonies. One of the best examples of walls being used for defense can be found at Dos Pilas, where they were built in haste from the materials that comprised the religious buildings. Defenders constructed two concentric walls to create a 20- to 30m-wide (66 to 99ft) killing zone. When the attackers breached the gates, they were caught between two walls and became easy targets for the defenders on the inner wall. Archeologists have dug out numerous projectile points at that location, while burials of decapitated adult males were found just outside the walls. This proves just how effective and bloody the Maya defensive tactics and fortifications could be. But as it was already mentioned, in the end they weren't enough to save the city.

Other cities that shared a similar fate with Dos Pilas made crude, rubble barricades in times of urgency. Of course, those types of defensive structures were less efficient. Another type of protective structures were wooden palisades, sometimes reaching to heights of 9m (30ft). If they weren't built in haste because of impending attack, the palisades could have been covered with plaster to prevent them from catching on fire easily. During the Terminal Classic and Postclassic periods, there was another important leap in fortification systems. Walls became fitted with wider ramparts, parapets, and interior walkways. This came about due to the increased usage of archers in wars since they could fire from greater distances. From the tops of the walls, defenders could use the threat of archers to keep attackers further away. During this period, defensive systems became more complex, being created in multiple rings of defense, with the last ring protecting the sacred and most important city center. But besides making defenses go deeper inwards, some of the cities created smaller forts outside the city's limits. Those were used as the first perimeter of defense; to lessen the chance of surprise attacks. Yet no matter how complex and efficient these defenses were, it seems that in the end, nothing could really protect the Maya cities from the troubles of war. All of them eventually suffered defeat.

The Maya continued to try to prevent those fatal outcomes. Yet another way they tried to improve the defensive capabilities of their settlements was by utilizing landscape. This became more common in the Postclassic era, especially in the Highlands. There, many cities and fortifications were erected on hilltops, which made access to them difficult. Sometimes the only way to get near the city was a narrow path, easily controlled by the defenders. Other times, a city was surrounded by a ravine which could be crossed only by a plank bridge that defenders could remove. But fortifications like these became more of a citadel type, used primarily for defenses and not as dwellings. In the Lowlands, the main use of natural defenses were islands on the lakes and coasts, which couldn't be crossed without a canoe or a ship. The Spaniards have also mentioned the use of traps as defensive measures. One example of that was the Maya trying to lure the Conquistadors onto a narrow pathway and then cutting off the exits. The idea was to defeat them in a high space where their horses were unable to maneuver, making them easy targets for both archers and spearmen.

Another important question that needs to be answered is why warfare was so important for the Maya. This is best explained by analyzing the types of wars they waged, or more precisely by determining what the main goal was to be achieved by the attackers. Most commonly, the Maya states went to war in the attempt to expand their territories and influence. This was done to economic gain, mostly through control of trade routes and resources, and additionally to attain political advancement. Wars could be motivated by the desire to defeat an ally or a vassal of an enemy state, by quests to remove a dynasty, by the urge to improve the political strength of one's own state, or even by revenge in some cases. Added benefits of successful wars were the tributes paid by conquered cities. Revenge sometimes gave war other dimensions, transforming a confrontation from a territorial conflict into a mission of destruction. This was less common, as it obviously didn't yield as many benefits as conquering. If it was done, it was usually a culmination of years of animosity and hostility. The best example of this was Dos Pilas, which was destroyed without any signs that the attackers had tried to conquer or subdue it. Another example of a destruction war was when Chichén Itzá annihilated one of its competitors in maritime trade. There was no motivation for revenge but for the simple calculation that a competitor needed to be destroyed without giving any chance of later revival; recovery would have been possible if it was merely turned into a vassal city.

But gains and revenge weren't the only reasons for the Maya to go to war. Another crucial motivation was religion and rituals. As we have learned, it was an important part of the rulers' image to be presented with captives to be used in the ceremonial sacrifices needed to please the gods. Catching those victims was certainly one of the motivators for Maya wars. Though it should be emphasized that unlike previously believed by archeologists, this wasn't the main cause of war. With "common" wars being fought regularly, most states didn't lack the captives for those needs. But in some cases, when Maya kings needed to prove themselves and acquire sacrificial victims, it could lead to conflict, though not likely full-scale war. And though religion wasn't often a cause of war, it certainly was commonly used to justify it. The Maya would often look at the night sky, looking at the movement of Venus, which was associated with war. Wars were typically waged when it was visible in the sky. Indeed, these wars have been marked with a star war glyph on the monuments and in texts. This meant that the war was sanctioned as a divine mission, similarly to the crusades or jihad. It was commonly used as justification for territorial warfare, making so-called "Star Wars" not-uncommon occurrences.

Chapter 7 – Economy of the Maya civilization

So far, in previous chapters, it could be noticed that the economy was one of the important drives of the Maya civilization. It was a base which propelled their polities from chiefdoms to states, it allowed the expansion of culture and great architectural achievements, because of it, wars were started and ended. Even the Maya realized how important the economy was to them, especially in the late Postclassic period when their society turned to rapid commercialization. To fully understand the Maya history, development, and culture, one has to get to know how their economy worked as well. It started from its early tribal backgrounds of hunting and foraging, then switched to farming when the Maya ancestors chose a sedentary way of life. Since then, the foundation of the Maya economy was agriculture. Early on, during the Preclassic age, the Maya figured out that water management was the key for both better and more reliable harvests. That is why they built wells, canals, and in some extreme cases like Kaminaljuyú, created massive irrigation systems. Besides those, it was common to create water reservoirs from natural and manmade subterranean caves, as well as quarry pits that were lined with clay to make them more watertight. In some cases, in Yucatan, the Maya even deepened the natural water-retaining depressions and cultivated water lilies to slow down the water evaporation.

Droughts weren't the only problem the Maya faced in agriculture. Flooding and heavy rains were also troubling, but the canals and other water management systems also drained water. Where there was no need for canals they used the drain and raise technique, where the fields were covered in a network of drainage ditches which took away the excess water, while simultaneously earth dug up from the ditches was piled up on the same fields, elevating them from the floodplain. Another problem faced by the Maya farmers was maintaining the fertility of the soil. They used various techniques for that, from planting complementary species near each other, like beans and maize, to using fertilizer made from household refuse, and crop rotation. The Maya farmers also used swidden agriculture methods, but this was primarily used to create new fields. And although altogether these approaches to preservation of soil show a real understanding of agriculture, it wasn't enough to maintain food supplies when the population grew too much. Thus, many of the fertile fields were overused and depleted by the time the Classic era was coming to an end.

Nonetheless, the Maya agriculture endured, while farmers searched for new fertile soils in which to plant their crops. Those can be divided into two major groups, food crops, and export or cash crops. Major food crops were maize, manioc, squash, sweet potato, papaya, pineapple, avocado, tomatoes, chili peppers, and common beans. Beside those, the Maya also grew some medicinal herbs in smaller house gardens. And although the food was sometimes traded, main trade income would have come from the cash crops. Most important of those was probably cacao, which was highly sought-after by the higher classes for making of chocolate beverages. Cacao was also linked to the gods, and it even served as currency to a certain extent. Another important export crop was cotton which, thanks to the climate, grew well in the Yucatan region. Unlike cacao, cotton was most commonly first turned into a finished textile produce before being exported, and it was important source of income. A third major cash crop was agave plant which was used to produce hemp fibers for inexpensive commoners' clothing and sandals, as well as strong ropes. Additionally, they cultivated tobacco, which was used for both religious rituals and individual pleasure. Despite the development of agriculture, hunting and foraging also remained sources of food and income for the Maya.

Animals that were hunted ranged from large deer, through peccaries and monkeys, to quail and partridge. They also hunted for crocodiles and manatees. For larger game, the Maya hunters used mainly spears and bows, while for monkeys and birds they used blowguns. They also employed traps which were mainly used to catch tapirs and armadillos, as well as turtles and iguanas, who in addition to meat were a source of highly-favored eggs. As with farming, not all animals were hunted for food. Jaguars, macaws, and quetzals were primarily hunted for their feathers, claws, pelts, and teeth, which were in high demand by the nobles for clothing and accessories. That made them valuable trade items. But the jungle was also suitable for foraging, giving the Maya more food like mushrooms, sometimes hallucinogenic, and various berries, as well as greens like tree-spinach and radish-like root plants. Rainforests were also sources of medicinal herbs and spices, like oregano and allspice. They also gathered vanilla pods, both for flavoring and fragrance, sometimes even cultivating vanilla vines deep in the tropical jungle. Of course, the Maya also fished, both on sea coasts, and further inland, and on lakes and rivers. They caught shrimp, lobster, various shellfish, and fish. The ocean-sourced fish were sometimes salted and traded as a delicacy to interior regions.

All of the previously listed economic activities are fairly common around the world, so it's not surprising that the Maya practiced them as well. What can be a bit of a shock is that animal husbandry was never truly developed by the Maya. They only domesticated dogs, for hunting and as pets, while turkeys and Muscovy ducks were only semi-domesticated. In some cases, they would capture and hold a deer for a while before eating it later. But the Maya did practice beekeeping, especially in Yucatan. There they would make hives from the hollowed tree trunks, which they plugged on the end. Honey was important as the only known sweetener to the Maya, which made it both important part of the diet and a valuable trade item. But more important than sweet honey was salt, necessary to maintain life. And although nearly all the Maya that lived on the coast were producing it, Yucatan salt was most valued and produced in much larger quantities. It was sought-after even by the Central Mexican nobility. Another product that was in some cases reserved for the nobility was alcoholic beverages, mostly consumed during feasts and rituals. The most famous examples of Maya alcoholic drinks, and which are still made today, are balché, a mild liquor, and chicha, a maize beer.

The second major branch of the Maya economy was crafting and artisanal work. The range of those products, as well as skills of the makers, went from simple and crude to exquisite artistry. And though most of them were commoners, highly skilled artisans often rose the middle class, while even some of the nobles practiced forms of craftwork. Of all the products those craftsmen made, ceramics were probably the most important for the economy. First of all, ceramics were essential in everyday life; everything from cooking pots to storage jugs. These goods varied in quality, beauty, and shape. But, if they were painted and adorned, they served a more ornamental role, like vases and figurines. Then ceramics became a rather important trade commodity, highly-valued by the nobility. Importance of ceramics in the Maya society can be further demonstrated by the fact that they developed a means of mass producing it. They created molds from which they many copies of the same product, from which even artistic figurines were made. And if needed, the "blank canvas" of those products could be embellished or individualized through painting or adding handmade details. More important is the fact that mass production meant ceramics were getting easier to make, cheaper, and more available. They were useful in trade, for both carrying other goods, and as an item of trade in and of itself.

Those who painted the ceramics, depending on their skill and the quality of their work could in some cases even be considered artistic, while others are more artisans and simple painters. They all used a variety of brushes and tools that resemble the wooden stylus of the ancient Near East. Those, with other tools and weapons, were another important part of the craftsmanship of the Maya pre-industrial workers. The toolmakers' main resources were, as was already mentioned, obsidian and chert. Those tools were part of the ceramics trade, but also necessary as a consumer good. Toolmakers also made wooden weaving battens, handles, and levers, while bones were used for needles and fishing hooks. For heavier work tools, such as chisels, scrapers, grinding stones, and axes they used basalt. Those types of tools were commonly used and are found at all sites. But precise work tools, like micro-drills needed for the finest lapidary work, are found only at the elite quarters of the urban centers. This indicates that those artisans were either of noble descent or were held in high regard by the ruling class. Again, it shows how some parts of the craft industry were appreciated in the Maya society, at least in the Classical period.

By the Postclassic period, around 13th century C.E., toolmakers embraced a new technology and resource for their products. They started using copper to create axes, fishing hooks, and tweezers. This debunks one of the most common myths that the Maya didn't have any knowledge of metallurgy. The truth is that copper wasn't that much better than the stone tools they created. And, in their region there weren't any copper mines, but obsidian, chert, and basalt were present in abundance. The only metal they had was gold, and it was panned in small quantities in the Highlands. Most of their precious metals were traded from the southern parts of Mesoamerica, and those were usually imported as finished products. While there were some gold and silver artifacts that were most likely created by the Maya craftsmen, it seems that they didn't develop many such skills. They focused on working with precious stones, which were also abundant in the Maya homeland. Jade, serpentine, turquoise, and pyrite were most commonly used. From those, they fashioned jewelry, home decorations, figurines, and other pieces of art. Pyrite was specifically used to create divining mirrors. Of these, jade was both the most precious and also the hardest to work with. Historians today find it remarkable that the Maya artisans were able to work with jade without any metal tools and think that great skill and dedication was needed to produce high quality from that particular stone. The Maya craftsman also used red shells and bones to make jewelry and other artwork. All of these products were highly valued in trade.

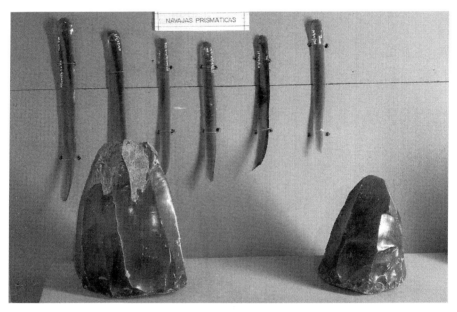

Raw obsidian and obsidian blades crafted by Maya artisans. Source: https://commons.wikimedia.org

Another tradable item was cotton clothing. As mentioned, cotton was grown by the Maya farmers, but expert weavers did the processing. They used a variety of complicated techniques to create pieces of cotton fabric used to make clothing. It was reserved for the nobles, in some cases even used as tributes and gifts to the royalty. They were adorned with various abstract symbols, most often connected with cosmological and religious motifs. In some cases, feathers were also woven into the clothing, which was commonly colorful. They used dyes made from plants, insects, and shells, and the most commonly used colors were dark blue, red, purple, and black-purple. Weavers also produced cotton tapestries and brocades, as decoration and as art. All of this indicates that the textile enterprise was another important part of the Maya economy. Of course, that type of highly-priced cotton textile was reserved for the elite. In some rare cases the Maya commoners had clothing made of lesser quality homespun cotton, but more often they wore simple loincloths made from various hemp fibers. Another type of common attire was pounded bark cloth, which some historians argue was used only for ceremonial occasions.

A more interesting use of pounded bark material was for making a crude version of paper. This Mesoamerican paper, referred to as such because its exact origin is unknown, was made usually from wild fig bark which was boiled in maize water, treated with lime or ash, then peeled in thin leaves. Those leaves were laid crisscross on a wooden board, then beaten with a stone into a single sheet of paper. Finishing with a thin layer of plaster ensured that the final product was smooth enough to write on. The most notable use of this paper was for writing books and codices, which were unfortunately almost all destroyed by the Spaniards. But Mesoamerican paper was also likely used in rituals, and for keeping records of trading, tributes, and other state business. The Maya made other products from plant fibers and vines, most notably mats, baskets, and fans. Mats were connected with the ruler and with authority, making them at least symbolically important. Baskets were in most cases used as an everyday item for carrying various items, but in some situations, they were linked with ceremonies of sacrificial offerings to the gods.

After listing all the important products of two major branches of the Maya economy, it is time to turn our attention to the third branch which created nothing except profit. Of course, this branch is trading. By now it should be clear that a lot of Maya life revolved around trade, and historians think it was the most important "motor" that drove the advance and growth of the Maya civilization. Most of the strongest Maya states drew strength from the control of the trade routes, and they often fought for them. But trade also facilitated connection with both other regions of the Maya homeland, and also with other surrounding nations. As a result, the Maya weren't only exchanging goods, but also ideas, technologies, and beliefs. That is one of the reasons why the historians have been so focused on the long distance, interregional trade, that connected present-day New Mexico with Panama and Columbia. The Maya held the central position of that trade. They exported and imported nearly all the resources and products mentioned in this chapter, except food. They also imported resources not commonly found in their homeland like silver, gold, pearls, copper, rubber, turquoise, etcetera. But the Maya traders also played a role of middle-man in trade between northern and southern Mesoamerica, and in some cases even larger areas.

This is not to say that a single Maya merchant traveled from Panama to New Mexico. Long-distance trading was done in stages, like a relay race, where the goods would be carried by a single trader only for one part of the route. Yet, the Maya merchants did have an enclave in early classic Teotihuacan, 1600km (1000mi) from their homeland. And this close connection with central Mexico continued when the Aztecs became the major power in the region. Another important factor of interregional trade is that it reinforced the authority and prestige of the ruler, as the royal family most often controlled the vital resources traded by the Maya. So, when the Maya traded for luxury goods, acquired products went to the ruler, and in some cases the highest elite. That way the king and the nobles were the ones profiting the most from this type of trade. Of course, this wasn't the only kind of commerce. There was also a regional trade, between the Maya themselves. As it was already mentioned, not all regions of the Maya homeland were suitable for producing everything or had access to the same raw resources. That is why there was a need for cities to complement each other with various products. Best example would be that the exchange of obsidian products for salt between the Highlands and Yucatan states. These trade connections were obviously strong and so frequent that they kept the Maya tightly connected in one rather homogenous civilization.

This was facilitated by the rulers, who of course benefited from trade. They sponsored and organized markets in their city centers, trying to attract more people to trade on their land. Although archeologists aren't completely sure, it is likely that the large and permanent Maya markets were under strict government control. Its officials enforced rules, settled disputes, and of course collected taxes. Naturally, these central markets were also used by the local population to acquire the goods they needed, and it is also likely that smaller and less permanent local markets existed which were used for local trade. This third type of trading was used between neighbors, trading among themselves for produce they lacked. All the families were focused and specialized on one type of production, so they created surpluses which they traded for items that they were missing. This type of trade wasn't that profitable and wasn't done by the professional merchants. It was the common people who bartered among each other. It is also likely that it wasn't as regulated as the higher levels of trade. Yet it was important for the survival of the local communities and the common citizens.

By getting familiar with all three levels or types of trading, as well as the reach of the merchants, it is possible to make a general idea of how the Maya trade network looked. But there is another important issue regarding this network yet to be discussed: the transport of goods. The first method to develop, and more commonly employed in the local and partially in regional trade, was overland transport. Without any animals to facilitate land transport, it was all done by human porters. In some cases, they carried the goods on their back, in other two or more of them would carry a litter. These were also used to transport richer travelers. These carriers used trails and sacbeob when they existed on their routes. Relay teams were used to make the transport faster and easier, especially if the cargo was heavy or if the final destination was further away. But in any case, this type of transportation was rather hard, slow and in essence inefficient. That is why the Maya used waterborne transport whenever they could. It was first done using rivers, connecting the inland cities. But as shipbuilding technology improved, and the Maya commerce began to expand further and further away, they also started to use the sea for transport.

Maya depiction of a man in a canoe. Source: https://commons.wikimedia.org

For that, they used canoes, which by the beginning of the 16th century were about 2.5m (8ft) wide and as long as galleys, according to the accounts of Columbus' son. Their vessels were fitted with palm canopies to protect passengers and goods. And in the same description, it was stated that the Maya canoes could carry up to 25 people on board, which means they carried substantial amounts of cargo as well. That fact also pushed the expansion of the sea trade, which led to the rise of up to 150 ports on the Yucatan coast in the Post-Classic period. This, of course, caused a lot of the Classical era Lowlands trade centers to lose their power and importance. But throughout the periods some aspects of trade didn't change much. One of those was a payment system. It seems that the most common "currency" was cacao beans. They were deemed valuable, and there were some reports of counterfeiting them by filling an empty cacao shell with dirt. Yet exactly how the Maya governments controlled its value and protected the cacao as a type of money remains an enigma for historians. Besides paying with cacao, it seems some other luxury items were also used for payments, also with what seem to have been fixed market values. These were jade beads and oyster shells. Later on, with the introduction of metals, the Maya merchants also started using gold and copper. Of course, barter was also a common form of payment, especially in local markets.

To ensure the trade deals would go through without problems the Maya merchants even created contracts, especially for larger or more valuable exchanges. These contracts might have been only oral, since they were sealed by public drinking. This may have given a rise to a culture of traders' integrity, as the Spaniards have observed that the Maya merchants were rather honorable. They also noted that usury didn't exist among them. All these factors combined demonstrate that the Maya trade was quite complex and very organized, not at all primitive as was once thought. That, combined with developed agricultural and craft production makes it apparent that the Maya had a robust and diverse economy. It shows yet another part of the Maya civilization that was thriving, pushing it to new greatness.

Chapter 8 – The Maya achievements in arts and culture

The highly developed and rather complex Maya civilization managed to create stunning pieces of art, bearing witness to the level of sophistication that the Maya culture achieved. Their creations ranged from monumental and breathtaking architecture and monuments, through beautiful and finely made figurines, paintings and books, to the less tangible and equally amazing intellectual achievements. With those, the Maya left a clear mark on both Mesoamerican and global culture, giving yet another reason for present-day researchers and historians to focus on uncovering their stories and achievements. The first thing that caught their attention, of course, were grand buildings and ruins that were left, lost to the wild jungles. The question of who built those big structures was the mystery that initially attracted the historians to the Maya civilization. And it was a first step in dismantling the old prejudices of the natives being only barbaric primitive tribes. From the first glance, it was clear that no backward society could have ever built something like the Maya pyramids and temples. And the somewhat interesting fact is that the biggest examples of those structures actually comes from the Preclassic era, not the golden age. But though smaller in size, those buildings, maintaining their basic form and look, were built until the arrival of Spaniards.

Also, common types of structures were palaces, ceremonial platforms usually up to 4m (6.5ft) high, council houses, ball courts, tombs and acropolises, observatories, sweat baths, and ceremonial stairways. These were generally public buildings, except palaces, which were usually placed around a central city plaza. They played an important role in the religious and political life of every urban center, and those were adorned with various carvings and other types of decorations. And as they were built to last, those buildings were usually built out of limestone, but also other types of stone like marble, sandstone, and trachyte, depending on local availability. In areas where the stone wasn't as common, those buildings were built out of adobe clay, which was more typically used for the homes of commoners. For mortar they used limestone cement, while plaster was used to seal the exterior walls as it was easier to decorate. The Maya masons also mastered the technique of corbelled arches to create tall yet narrow doorways and domes. The reverse "V" shape of these arches, or vaults as they are also called, is one of the architectural hallmarks of the Maya, as almost none of the other civilization of Mesoamerica built them. Structures with these arches resembled their original thatched huts but were also better cooled which is an important advantage in the tropical climate. Also, the vaults made the buildings look more impressive from the outside, which was always an important factor for the Maya.

All these features are common among the Maya cities, distinguishing them from the rest of Mesoamerica. But some local differentiation in style existed, as well as certain evolution and development as time passed. Those were both caused by the availability of resources and different foreign influence, but also by the individual tastes of particular rulers. But no matter the fine details, there is no doubt that the Maya, in general, were capable and skilled masons, as their structures still stand tall and proud. Yet the details that are commonly considered to be their most beautiful feature were not done by them. There were specialized stone carvers which were tasked with creating those artistic masterpieces. They were usually carved in stucco, with scenes that were either taken from mythology or which celebrated the ruler. Often those two were interconnected, as the rulers were shown performing various rituals. But the Maya sculptors didn't only decorate the walls. They also used their skill to adorn lintels, altars, thrones, and most notably, stelae. And today historians praise their work not only for the sculpting skills of the Maya but also because those carvings are one of the major sources of information about the civilization's past.

Similarly, the murals and wall painting, usually done on the interior walls, also became important evidence of the Maya history. Though not many are saved, ones that are preserved today show us glimpses of the court life, ritual ceremonies, wars, and battles. Those scenes are painted with vivid and bright colors, which are a clear reminder that the Maya cities were rather colorful places. It the Classical era it was common for the wall paintings to have hieroglyphic text accompanying them, giving more detailed context to the scenes. And the skill level of the Maya painters is no lesser than that of the carvers. Besides sharing the similar, if not the same, imagery, they also share the same stylistic characteristics. Most notable of these is the naturalistic and rather realistic representation of places and humans. Yet in most of the artwork people, even the rulers, lack the individual traits that would distinguish their facial characteristics. Another fact that binds them is the fact that their main purpose was to celebrate and promote the rulers and their cults, which suggests that they were mostly commissioned by the royal families. Only in the Postclassic period, when the ruler cult was dying out, did the scenes focus more on religious and mythological topics, as well as on the noble lineages. But the fact remains that these artists worked only for the members of the elite, and most likely worked in patronage systems.

Not everything the artists created was as large as the wall decorations. Both painters and sculptors also worked on smaller items. Sculptors created many decorative masks, celts (axe heads), pendants, and figurines out of precious stones, most notably jade. Depending on their purpose, their themes changed. In some cases, they were made to represent a certain deity or mythological creature, while some of the celts were fitted with the representation of kings.

And most famous masks were usually death masks, without any specific facial features. As creations made of such expensive materials wouldn't have been as available to the less fortunate, the Maya sculptors also carved smaller wooden figurines and effigies. Again, main themes were the rulers, and even more often they are the representation of gods. On the other hand, the Maya painters worked on adorning various pottery products, but most notably vases and bowls. Their artwork was rather similar in every aspect to the murals, except in size. Themes remained connected to religion, rulers and court, done in a colorful pallet. And both paintings and sculptures retained naturalistic form and a sense of realism.

Copy of a Maya mural with restored colors. Source:
https://commons.wikimedia.org

Unlike other Maya artists, pottery makers weren't only focused on making objects of stunning beauty. They also had to focus on practicality and usefulness. Based on that idea, it is possible to separate the types of Maya pottery into two main groups. The first one would be ceremonial, made for the elite and for religious needs. That type of pottery was often polychrome, with a mixture of more than one mineral slip, and was often decorated with paintings. These vessels were also more elaborate in shape and form, adding a base flange, knobs in shape of animal or human heads, and mammiform-

or leg-shaped supports. Some of the vessels were shaped and decorated as human or animal heads. The Maya potters also made naturalistic figurines representing people doing various types of mundane activates. These were mostly painted, probably made for nobles, as they were likely to be costly. Utilitarian pottery was more commonly used by the lower classes, as they were cheaper and less finely-made. In contrast to ceramics made for the elites, these were monochrome, simple in shape and form, and without many decorations, if they had any at all. The main focus of pottery makers, in this case, was to make them useful in everyday life, while not being too concerned with beauty. And the already mentioned mass-produced pottery, by using a mold, was usually created for commoners, not the elite. For one, it was cheaper and more available, but also the nobles liked their possessions to be more unique, representing their position in the society.

The same role of social status symbols was assigned to clothing and jewelry, which also represented the skillful artwork of the Maya artisans. But these will be discussed in a later chapter about the daily life of the Maya, as those art forms are better suited for describing their lifestyle than artistic and cultural achievements. On the other hand, books and writing could be seen as the pinnacle of the Maya cultural achievements. As was mentioned before, the books were written on crude bark paper, covered with a thin layer of plaster. There were probably thousands and thousands of Maya codices, as their books are more commonly called, written during their long history, yet today only four remain, since the Spaniards burned them as blasphemous and evil. All four books are linked to rituals, religion, mythology, astronomy, and astrology. But it's not unlikely that among many others that were burned were books about their history and past, about their scientific and philosophical findings, poetry, and stories. Alas, we will never know for sure. What is striking is the beauty of the books, in which illustrations complemented texts. Those drawings, in similar style to the paintings, are colorful and naturalistic. In the four remaining codices, they represented gods and mythological heroes, which isn't surprising considering their theme. Hieroglyphic writing is done in one color, mostly red or black. Even those glyphs can on their own be seen as art motifs, as they are no less stunning or interesting than the illustrations. And similar to modern books, the pages of the Maya codices were protected with covers made out of tree bark or pelts, in some cases even jaguar skin. In that aspect, every book represents a singular artistic creation worthy of any great civilization.

But books and other Maya texts for that matter represent more than just art. They convey a message that can transcend both time and space. And developing a writing system is a step of utmost importance in creating a developed civilization. Unfortunately for historians, not only did the Spaniards destroy the books, but they also destroyed the Maya literacy, at least when it comes to their own hieroglyphs. That is one of the reasons why for a long time historians and archeologists debated about Maya script, with skeptics claiming that it's not really a writing system, but rather religious illustrations or symbols, similar to Christian icons. Of course, through long and hard work by many generations of linguists and Mayanists, there is no longer any doubt that the Maya have indeed had a fully developed writing system, one which could transcribe everything they spoke. According to some researchers, the Maya are the only civilization in pre-Columbian Mesoamerica that developed a fully functional script, yet this claim is uncertain and could be disproven if any other Mesoamerican script is deciphered.

The origin of the Maya writing system isn't exactly clear. Some historians believed that the Maya adopted their script from the Olmecs. The Olmecs, mentioned earlier as one of the oldest civilizations in Mesoamerica, had a writing system that is currently being studied by researchers. However, that system does not show signs of the full development evident in Maya hieroglyphs. One reason this theoretical connection between Olmec and Maya script is the similarity in the glyphs and the style of writing. Others think the

Maya developed their writing system on their own. One of the reasons for that is that the first signs of Maya proto-writing date to around 400 B.C.E., a time when the Olmec's civilization was near its end. And, the first recognizable scripts date to around 50 B.C.E., when the Olmecs were long gone. Yet, even if the latter theory is right, it is likely that the Olmecs at least slightly influenced the Maya script. Whatever is the truth, today we can say with certainty that the Maya writing system was a mixture of a phonetic and logographic script. This means that certain glyphs represent syllables consisting of a consonant and vowel, which combined together could spell out any word. While other glyphs represented on their own the whole word. Today most of these glyphs have been translated, with new discoveries being made constantly. Thanks to this important work, historians can now decipher and translate almost all Maya texts.

Pages from one of the Maya codices. Source: https://commons.wikimedia.org

Text wasn't written only in books, but on just about anything; from walls and monuments to a variety of pottery, celts, and stone tools. On bigger objects and walls, they told a story, conveyed a complex message about achievements of the king or details of a certain ritual.

On smaller objects, like jars or vases they were simple tags, marking either their maker or their owner. They were even found in permanent markets, marking areas or stands with the type of products that were being sold there. This widespread use of writing, especially on objects not related to the royalty and the elite, brought up a question of general literacy among the pre-conquest Maya. Of course, there is no way to be exactly sure, but some historians argue that literacy, at least a basic one, was rather widespread among all the people. Otherwise, there wouldn't be any point in writing on common objects and places. Full literacy, however, was limited to the higher classes with their specially trained scribes, given that there were about 800 glyphs, of which about 500 were commonly used. But, as the Spaniards fought their cultural war against the Maya, they found one way to save at least part of their legacy, mythology, and traditions. This was for the Maya to learn to use the Latin alphabet and then transcribe some of their original works. Those kinds of books were not always seen as evil by the Spanish clergy, and some managed to survive, though it is reasonable to assume that the Europeans discouraged the Maya from their preservation efforts. The most famous example of Maya literature transcribed into Latin is the Popol Vuh, which was most likely written in the second half of the 16th century.

Maya intellectual and cultural achievements didn't end with writing. They were also superb astronomers, who probably started to gaze at the stars so they could praise their gods. It's precisely because of this that some of the commonly-found buildings in all major Maya cities were observatories. After a while, the Maya observers started noting certain patterns, noting them with tremendous accuracy. With nothing more than their naked eyes, strings, and sticks they calculated that the revolution of Venus around the Sun took 584 days. Today's astronomers measured it to be exactly 583.92 days, making the Maya margin of error about 0.01%. Of course, they also tracked movements of other celestial bodies, which was used to align important buildings, like temples or palaces, with the position of the

Sun on the horizon at the solstices and equinoxes, as well as with the zenith passages. But more commonly, those movements and positions of celestial bodies were used for divination and fortunetelling. So, in a way, the Maya sky observers were a mix of astrologers and astronomers. One example of this is looking at the position of Venus before going to war, as it was considered that fighting without that planet in the night sky would anger the gods and bring bad luck. Going further, they also created their own zodiac, dividing the sky into sections and constellations. It is likely they used it like all ancient societies, and like it is still used today, to predict fortunes and future events. Yet exact details on the number and positioning of the Maya constellations, their celestial signs, and their position in the night sky are unknown, and under constant debate among the experts.

From their ability to track the cycles of the night skies, as well as other observations in nature, the Maya were able to become excellent timekeepers. For that purpose, they used an intricate system which combined three different calendars. But this system shouldn't be seen as a pure creation of the Maya. Almost all Mesoamerican nations used it, and it likely originated from the Olmecs, though that has not been conclusively proven. Thus, phrases like "the Maya calendar" aren't correct, and they should be substituted by "the Mesoamerican calendar." The shortest of the three calendars the Maya used was called the Tzolk'in, and it was 260 days long, divided into 13 "months" which numbered 20 days. Researchers were unable to find any astronomical significance for this period of time, but it has been suggested it was linked with the period of human pregnancy, which usually lasts for about 266 days. This connection is still used by the present-day Maya women. Another possible link is maize cultivation, giving an approximate time when to plant and harvest this important crop. But, its main use seems to be for divination and fortune-telling. There is evidence for this in the Maya codices, which contain Tzolk'in almanacs. Those were used by the diviners to guide the rulers before making any important decisions. Today the Maya still use it to pick a date for a wedding or a business trip, so it is not unlikely that the commoners in the past did the same.

Less religious, but more practical, would be the second calendar the Maya used called the Haab'. This calendar was 365 days long, coinciding with a solar year. It was divided into 18 months of 20 days, with an extra five days added at the end. Because of its structure, the scholars today call it the vague year calendar. The main use of Haab' was for agriculture, as the name of the months suggests a seasonal division of the calendar. Water and dry months were grouped together, as well as the earth months and the maize months. The 5 days added at the end of every year were called Wayeb' and were considered very unlucky throughout Mesoamerica. It was believed that during these five days, connections between the underworld and the mortal realms were heightened. Nothing was preventing the gods or other creatures from coming into the world and causing death and destruction. This is why during these days, the Maya performed various rituals to prevent the destruction of their world and to ensure coming of the new year.

Using two rather different calendars could have confused the Maya, and so they found a way to avoid this. They created the so-called calendar round date, by combining both the Tzolk'in and Haab' dates. That date would repeat itself after 52 Haab' or 72 Tzolk'in years, making a single calendar round. But there was still one more problem left with those two calendars, and that is measuring the long periods of time, since it became possible to confuse specific dates within different calendar rounds. This can be compared with the form in which we sometimes write our dates, e.g. "5.3.18." When writing the date in this way, we could be referring to May 3, 2018, or to May 3, 1918. To avoid that confusion, the Maya used the cyclical Mesoamerican long count calendar, which is often wrongly named the Maya calendar. The base of this calendar was Haab', with cycles starting from one day (k'in), growing to one month (winal) of 20 days, to one year (tun) made of 18 winals. A tun was 360 days and did not include the unlucky 5 Wayeb', which weren't counted as a true part of the year. The cycles continue, with the k'atun cycle being 20 tun, or years, long, following with b'ak'tun cycle lasting 20 k'atuns, or about 394 years. The scale continues, with every new cycle lasting 20 times more than the last. The last, 9th cycle called alautun lasts a little bit over 63 thousand years. The Maya themselves usually stopped at b'ak'tun when they inscribed their dates. That is why their Long Count dates are marked by series of 9 numbers, with first one representing b'ak'tun and last one representing k'in. Modern scholars note these dates in the same way, for example, January 22nd, 771 C.E., would be written down 9.17.0.0.0, with every number representing a single cycle.

Those cycles are being counted from the Maya mythological creation of the world which, transcribed to the Gregorian calendar, is dated to August 11^{th,} 3114 B.C.E. And, similarly to the end of the Haab' cycle, the Maya revered every other important cycle. Misinterpretation of the nature of Maya traditions and nature of the Long Count calendar led to now infamous 2012 "end of the world" media frenzy. According to some Maya text, the world we're currently living is actually the fourth iteration, with the previous three ending after 13 b'ak'tuns. And on December 21th of 2012 C.E., the 13th b'ak'tun from 3114 B.C.E., was coming to an end. This led some people to interpret this as the Maya prophecy of the world ending on that date, though this was not explicitly mentioned. It is possible that the Ancient Maya would have seen this date as religiously important, but there are no clear signs that would see it necessarily as a beginning of the apocalypse. It is more likely that for them that date was just another end of a cycle in their calendar. They would likely have performed a ritual or a ceremony to pray to the gods for good fortune in the new cycle. The cyclical nature of their calendars influenced the way the Maya thought about history and nature around them. Everything had its beginning and an end; nothing was permanent. And everything was repeating.

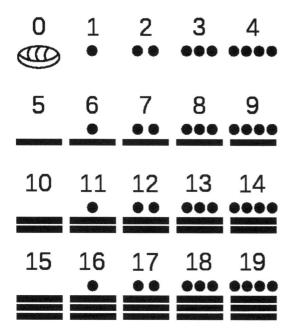

Example of Maya numerals. Source: https://commons.wikimedia.org

One of the significant concept in all three calendars that Maya used was the use of the number 20, with months lasting 20 days, and in the Long Count calendar cycles also being based on 20, with the exception to this rule being a tun made of 18 winals. This may seem strange to most of the people today as our numerical system is the positional decimal numeral system, meaning it is based on number 10. But the Maya, as well as most Mesoamericans, used the vigesimal positional numeral system, based on the number 20. The Maya had only three numeric symbols. Dot represented number 1, the horizontal bar was 5, and shell glyph represented a 0. With those three they would write out any number from 0 to 19. For example, 16 would be three stacked bars on top of each other with a single dot above them all. And if the Maya wanted to go above that, they added another line above, which would mean that numbers in that line would be multiplied by 20. For example, 55 would be written with two dots in the upper line, representing 2x20, and in the bottom line would be three bars, which would be 15. And the Maya could add lines as much as they wanted, with every line being multiplied once again by 20. Thus, the third line would be multiplied by 400 and fourth by 8000.

Though this base 20 system is interesting, more important is the Maya use of zero. Similar to both the calendar and numerical system, the shell glyph 0 was also used in all of Mesoamerica, and the exact origins of the glyph remain a mystery. Some think it was created by the Olmecs, while others attribute it to the Maya, but it may also be from some other Mesoamerican civilization thriving in last millennia B.C.E. The shell glyph was first detected in the Long Count dates from the 1st century B.C.E., where it was a placeholder that represented the absence of particular calendrical count, but it is likely that it was created before that. By 4th century C.E., it had evolved into a proper numeral that was used to perform calculations. And it was used for writing numbers; for example, 40 would be two dots on the second line, and a shell glyph on the bottom. Today this system sounds confusing and it seems that it requires a lot of math to use, but in reality, it was rather practical. Sources tell us that the Maya merchants, using easily transportable beans or kernels as placeholders, could write and calculate large quantities, making their system rather efficient. This seems especially so when compared to the alphabetical systems of ancient Greeks and Romans. And it is yet another sign of how advanced and capable the Maya civilization was, despite being thought of as barbaric for a long time.

Chapter 9 – Religion and rituals in the Maya society

Religion played an important part in almost all ancient societies; the Maya were no exception. It permeated every part of life, from the everyday troubles and hopes of the commoners, to matters of trade, agriculture, and economy, and to the state matters of wars and the cult of the rulers. Everything was guided and influenced by the omens and foretelling of both the future and the past, rooted in the religious beliefs of the Maya. That is why men of faith were an important part of their society. The first type of these holy men to appear in the Maya society were the shamans. Their origins can be traced to pre-civilized society of the Maya ancestors. They played a crucial role in establishing the basics of the calendars and the world order through their tracking of nature and the stars. They used that kind of knowledge to predict rains, a proper time for planning the crops, cure illnesses with herbs and, of course, perform divination rituals. Also, shamans in those early days represented the link with the ancestors, as well as the gods. They held a decent amount of power and prestige at the time. But with rising complexity of the forming Maya civilization most of those early shamans started to transform into the elite class of religious full-time specialists we now call priests. Yet the role of shamans was not entirely extinct, since many commoners took on that call in their local communities. They performed similar roles as before, but their reach was only on a local level, tending to the need of their fellow men.

In contrast to the shamans, priests, now members of the nobility, were responsible for the religious well-being of the entire state. They managed the calendars, divination for more important state affairs, books about both the past and the future, and public rituals and ceremonies. All those activities and responsibilities were linked with the prosperity and success of both the ruler and entire state. With that kind of power and importance, priests gained substantial political and social power. And as the number of political and government offices was limited, many of the younger elite and royal children saw those functions as a way to stay close to the status they were born into. But being of noble descent wasn't enough to become a priest, as all new acolytes had to pass a period of learning and training to become fully pledged priests. Then they would put on their elaborate and stunning robes and, through the many public rituals they conducted, they inspired awe, admiration, and ultimately obedience of the masses to both the state and even more so to the king. At the same time, they advised their rulers, helping them choose a path and lead their polities into the future.

Yet the importance of the priests in religious matters was overshadowed by none other than the king they advised. The ruler was also the chief priest, not only tasked with protecting his subjects from harm in the material world, but also from the suffering caused by the spirit realm. He would also perform various rituals and acts of divination, in an attempt to appease the gods, secure the success of his state, and ultimately to maintain order in the universe. As it was stated in previous chapters, this conjecture of religious and political power led to the forming of the ruler's cult, leading many to refer to the Maya rulers as the shaman kings. To emphasize this religious aspect of the royal rule, rulers wore robes with symbols of various deities, carried scepters and wore headdresses that were linked with some of the gods. Going even further, they claimed to be divine, either as the direct descendant of gods, or at least their voice on earth. Rulers also represented themselves as being in the center of the universe, connecting all the worldly plains, in an attempt to balance their forces. Ultimately, it is through the ruler and the rituals he performed that the supernatural powers merged with the activities and the lives of the humans, while at the same time binding religion and politics with an unbreakable bond.

Figurine of a Maya priest. Source: https://commons.wikimedia.org

For the Maya, the bond of supernatural plains and the material world also existed in nature. Most potent of those were mountains and caves, as they contained magical portals to otherworldly places. Mountains were usually connected to gods and the sky realm, they represented good, potency and were considered the origin of maize.

On the other hand, caves had a more dual role in religion. Since they led into the interior of the sacred mountains, they were also seen as places of possible potent fertility. At the same time, they were portals to the underworld, making them rather dangerous places. In Yucatan, cenotes played the similar role as the caves and they were considered as sacred, with the various offering being dropped into them. To harvest the supernatural powers of the places and transport them into their cities the Maya built pyramid temples, now one of the most famous aspects of their civilization. Of course, the pyramid represented the mountain. But in some cases, there were certain chambers inside the pyramids representing the caves. In one of the pyramids that chamber was an actual cave on top of which the temple was built. And on top of the pyramid, the Maya built what is the actual temple, the house of the god, as they called it. It was there that the kings and priests connected as directly as possible with the gods and their realm. Of course, not all temples were built on top of the pyramids, especially in smaller cities and villages. There they were more similar to the houses, representing more the connection with the ancestors. And they were seen as less supernaturally potent. The Maya also built small shrines, sometimes even on the very mountains they praised.

Of course, as the pyramid temples represented the most potent place for establishing connections with the gods, they were used for central public ceremonies. Those could be single-day events, or large celebrations that would last several nights and days. In those types of ceremonies, there would be several hundred or even thousands of people involved, most likely in the open plazas that were built in front of the temples. The ceremonies were led by the kings and priests, dressed to represent the gods, possibly even assuming their identities in the state of religious ecstasy. They would perform rituals leading the ceremony, in an attempt to connect with the supernatural forces, while the common people played music, danced, feasted, and drank. But not all ceremonies were state affairs. There was a whole range of ceremonies that involved commoners and local villages. Yet all of these ceremonies, in spite of being small, followed a similar pattern. The community would gather, eat and drink together, and dance while the shaman, dressed in symbols of the gods, tried to communicate with the gods and ancestors.

But no matter on what level those ceremonies were held, they had to be carried out in the correct way. First, the proper date had to be found through divination methods, then the ones who led the ceremonies, if not everyone involved, endured several days of abstinence and fasting, symbolizing spiritual purification. And most of the ceremonies included similar rituals, most commonly some form of divination, expelling the evil forces, dancing and music, and offerings to gods in various forms of sacrifices, bloodletting, food, or precious materials. All those rituals were usually accompanied by the burning of incense, whose smoke was supposed to more directly convey the message or the plea to the gods in the sky. It was also common for both shamans, as well as priest and kings, to consume various hallucinogenic substances to induce a trance-like state. Commoner population and local shamans for that purpose usually used strong alcoholic beverages and wild tobacco, which was more potent than the tobacco smoked today, while the "professional" high-ranking priests consumed various mushrooms, which were stronger hallucinogens and contained more psychoactive substances. All of the hallucinations and other types of experiences that the men of faith perceived during those altered states were conceived as communication with the gods. Those supernatural messages were either foretellings of the future or possible solutions and answers to the questions and problems that the gods were asked to help with.

In certain cases, it was required that clothing and objects used in a ceremony were new and unused. For those particular ceremonies, all of the items were made specially. Also important was the water, which was commonly used in many rituals. But for rituals that allowed the use of already used objects, clothing, and other equipment, the items still had to be purified with the smoke of burning incense. If the ceremony was of great importance, the Maya holy men would collect fresh "virgin" water from the caves to be used. Another important part of all major ceremonies was the music. From the archeological findings, it is obvious that percussion instruments were most common with various wooden drums, turtle shell drums, gourd rattles, and bone rasps. There were also flutes made from wood or clay, ocarinas, shell trumpets, and whistles. Music was vital for the opening procession of priests that usually started the ceremonies, but also for punctuating important parts and steps in the ritual. It is likely that the Maya felt that the music pleased the gods, facilitating the success of the ceremony. And of course, music was crucial for accompanying the ritual dances performed during the ceremony.

Undoubtedly for the Maya, those dances weren't entertainment, but rather serious religious practice. Dancers were dressed as the gods they tried to connect with, reenacting important scenes from their mythology. They felt they were almost becoming the deity in question, as well as gathering the life force that was in the nature around them, which was needed for interaction between the realms. Besides the clothing embedded with religious symbols, dancers also commonly carried scepters, banners, staffs, spears, rattles, and even live serpents. Maya art shows that the ritual dancers were among others kings, priests, nobles, and even warriors. But it is also likely that the local shamans danced during their rituals while trying to connect with the supernatural forces. Of course, dances differed, being specifically tailored for a certain ceremony and achieving a certain goal. Also, some of those dances were performed before the battles, praying for good fortune and victory. Dances were usually performed with more than one dancer. In some cases, one person was leading the dance or played a central role. Also, in some carvings, there are female dancers depicted, but it seems they weren't as common as males. But rituals, no matter how intricate and well thought out, weren't going to please the gods without the addition of offerings.

A mural of Maya musicians during a ceremony. Source:
https://commons.wikimedia.org

Ritual offerings to the gods varied according to the importance and urgency of the ritual. For less important, more common ceremonies and prayers, less precious and symbolic items would be enough, as evident from the offerings found in the sacred cenote of Chichén Itzá. But the Maya believed that what the gods actually craved was more of the life force. Thus, more often they offered food. The lowest on that scale were plant offerings, as it was considered that plant "blood" was potent. And as importance grew, so did the power and size of the being that was sacrificed, and whose blood was to be offered. For example, in a local village ceremony done by a common shaman, an offering of a bird or a small monkey would suffice. For a larger state ceremony led by a priest it is more likely they sacrificed a deer, or even several. Yet, no matter how big and powerful the animal was, human blood was seen as the most potent offering that could be made. This was done by the Maya of all classes, but again, when the members of the elite did it, it was most commonly done for the wellbeing of the entire state and its population. Most common source of the blood was the hand, but there are depictions of other body parts serving as the source, like the tongue or a cheek. There is also evidence that in some rituals kings drew blood from their penises, most likely in an attempt to pray for increased fertility. Blood, no matter of what origin, was most commonly soaked up with bark paper and burned or smeared onto the idols representing the gods.

But no matter how potent the blood of the self-inflicted bloodletting, it wasn't always enough. That is why the Maya practiced human sacrifice, which became one of the most notorious and well-known facts about their civilization and religion, and yet another reason why they were seen as savages for a long time. But for the Maya, it was a logical extension of offering to the gods, as there was nothing more powerful than an entire human life. It was the ultimate sacrifice. In no way was this an everyday event; it was used only for special occasions like crowning a new king, to bless his rule and connect him with the gods, or when a newly built temple needed to be dedicated. Human sacrifices were also used in times of great peril and trouble, be it drought, famine, disease outbreak, or a great and dangerous war. The most common victims were members of the enemy elite captured during the wars, as capturing prisoners was one of the major goals of the Maya warfare. Less often the sacrificed captives were from the lower classes, and even rarer was an enemy king. But in some dire cases there weren't any prisoners to be sacrificed, so the local population was used, though most likely starting from the commoners, then possibly working the way up to the elites if nothing else helped. And in these cases, it becomes unclear if the victims would volunteer themselves or if they were forcibly picked, or if it was a mix of both. And as most victims were war captives, men were more commonly sacrificed, but there is some evidence of both women and children being offered to the gods as well.

Though probably the earliest and most common way to execute the victim was a simple beheading, later the Maya sacrifices became more gruesome and bloody. They tied the captives to the poles and disemboweled them or executed them with a volley of arrows. In later periods, through influence from central Mexico, they started cutting out still beating hearts of the victims, offering the very core of human life to the gods. In Chichén Itzá, during the Postclassic era, they started performing sacrifices in which the prisoners were thrown into their sacred cenote. Victims were either killed by the 20m (65ft) drop or from drowning, perhaps weighed down by stones. Also, during those later periods, another practice was imported from the Central Mexican region. The Maya began painting their victim with blue sacrificial color. Finally, the famous Mesoamerican ball game, played on specially designed courts, was also used to perform human sacrifices. Exact details of the game, its purpose and use are under constant debate by historians, but it is clear that at least part of it was tied to the religion. Some think that teams who played against each other, in a game where the goal was to push the ball through a ring without using legs and arms, actually reenacted famous battles from both history and mythology. It is also suggested that the movements in the game represented the movements of the sun and the moon, while the court itself was seen as the representation of the Underworld or even the gateway to it.

A Maya vase depicting human sacrifice. Source: https://commons.wikimedia.org

It is suggested that the losing team, or at least its captain, was sacrificed to the gods when the game ended. That led researchers to conclude that the players were most likely, as were other victims, captives. Yet some evidence, mostly the depicted gear in some carvings, suggest that this may not always be the case. It is also possible that free people would volunteer for the game, knowing that they may end up being sacrificed, either because of their religious beliefs or more simply in an attempt to prove themselves and rise on the social ladder. But it should be pointed out that the ball game wasn't a purely religious event. It also contains certain elements of entertainment and competition. Some historians also suggested it could have been used to settle disputes between various communities that were part of the same polity. Whatever may be the truth, one thing was certain, sacrifice or not, everyone eventually dies, and death was an important part of the Maya religion. That is why the burial rituals have been seen as rather important. Common practice, no matter the social class, was to put maize or a jade bead into the mouths of the deceased, representing life itself. Alongside the body, various effigies were put, as well as an item that represented that person's life, for example, a book for a priest. Of course, if the deceased was more important and wealthier, he was also buried with various other treasures, even some sacrificed men, possibly to act as servants in the afterlife.

Another common practice was to wait a couple of days before burial, so the soul would have a chance to leave the body and continue its journey. Actual places where the dead were laid to rest differed both from the time period, and of course, from the class the deceased came from. Commoners were either buried on their own estates, in family graves or were left in caves. Some evidence also leads to a conclusion that certain "cemeteries" or burial grounds existed on the outskirts of larger cities, where the commoners were buried. Members of the elite and the royal families were buried in more elaborate tombs, with some of the significant rulers being buried in temples, in the city centers, so they could be revered as powerful ancestors. Even the commoner's graves were visited by their descendants on certain dates, who then burned incense and prayed to them in hope of guidance. This is yet another example of the Maya admiration of their ancestors, which was an important part of their religion. And from this chapter, it is obvious that the Maya religion was actually a complex system of rituals, ceremonies, and beliefs that guided their lives on an everyday basis. That intricate matrix of religious ideas, no matter how bloody or barbaric it may seem from our modern point of view, is yet another example of the complexity and advancement of the Maya civilization.

Chapter 10 – Myths, legends and the gods of the Maya

The Maya religion was polytheistic with an intricate and rich folklore of various myths, legends, and stories. Considering how important and complex their religious practices and rituals were, this shouldn't be much of a surprise. The Maya used these myths to explain and describe the world around them, to set certain guidelines in life, to give their universe some meaning. And to be able to understand both their religion and their society, one should first understand how their universe was divided. Vertically it was split into three realms. First was the Upperworld (Kan), the sky realm where the many of the gods lived and where most of their actions played out. According to some evidence, this realm was further divided into 13 ascending levels, and also it may have had a role similar to the Paradise of Christianity, into which warriors who fell in battle and women who died during childbirth were admitted directly. The second realm was the Underworld (Xibalba), which was an underground place that was also filled with gods and other supernatural creatures. It was imagined as a watery place, which was both the frightful realm of illness and decay, as well as source of great generative powers and fertility. It was divided into 9 layers, and here people who died a peaceful death were sent.

In between those two realms was Earth (Kab), the material world in which the Maya lived. It seems that they believed that the Middleworld, as it is also called, was the back of some kind of a reptile, either turtle or a caiman, that swam in the primordial sea, explaining the watery nature of the Underworld. This realm was divided horizontally into 5 directions of the world. East was the direction where the Sun was reborn, and its color was red. West was where the Sun died, and as such was the direction of the Underworld, or rather its entrance, represented with black. North was representing the noon and the sky, a place of the ancestors, and its color was white. South was the direction where the Sun wasn't visible as there, probably in the Underworld itself, it was fighting lords of Xibalba to be able to be born again. The color of the south was yellow. And the center was considered the fifth "direction", as it was the central axis of the universe, where the sacred World Tree connected all three realms, sharing their spiritual energy and allowing the transport of the souls and gods between them. It was symbolized by the cross. And when the rulers wanted to represent themselves as the center of the universe, they would adorn themselves with symbols of the World Tree, emphasizing their role as the connectors of the realms, directly linked to the gods.

But the question of gods in the Maya pantheon is rather complicated. So far, the researchers have singled out about 250 names of Maya deities, yet they don't think that all 250 of them were separate, distinct gods. Unlike most of the western pantheons, where gods are rather distinct and singular, the Maya deities were much more fluid. One Maya god could manifest different aspects of his power and nature, and for every manifestation, he would be named and represented differently. Some of the gods existed in quadripartite form, with every manifestation corresponding with four world directions and colors. Others existed in dual forms that represented opposites like good and bad, or young and old. Yet in the core of both cases, it would still be a single deity. On the other hand, many of the gods, in those manifestations, overlapped with each other. Their identities, roles, and functions could be mashed up together. This is why most researchers tend to think of the Maya pantheon being made out of clusters of gods, not individual deities. The fact that the Maya also believed that some gods were zoomorphic, capable to turn into animals, or combining human and animal elements also adds another layer of complexity to the pantheon. But some major deities have been identified and more clearly separated from each other.

The Maya god Itzamná. Source: https://commons.wikimedia.org

Among the most important of the major deities was Itzamná, who came the closest to being a supreme deity of the Maya. He was depicted as a wise old man, often as a scribe, sometimes with black obsidian mirrors used to read the past and the future. He was fundamentally a god of creation, playing an important role in creation. Itzamná was also attributed with the invention of books, thus the scribe depictions. As the Lord of the Gods, he presided over the heavens, both during the night and during the day. As such, representing an aspect of his fluidity, he has also been manifested as the principal bird deity called Itzam-Ye or Vuqub Caquix. Itzamná's importance is further underlined with the fact that he was the patron of the day Ahaw, which was the day of the king in the ritual Tzolk'in calendar. He has also manifested powers of healing illnesses, giving him the attributes of a medicine deity. He's married to one of the moon goddesses. Next in line of importance and power was the youthful god of the sun, K'inich Ahaw (the sun-faced lord). In some cases, he and Itzamná shared a duality of old and young, as K'inich Ahaw sometimes looks like a younger version of the creator god. As the sun god, he represented the day cycle and the solar energy that was vital for all natural life, which is why he was rather important to the farmers. But when the Sun went down to the Underworld he would transform into the Jaguar god, who through his battle for rebirth became the patron of war as well. As such the Maya kings often connected themselves with him.

Another god that was important to the farmers was the rain and storm god named Chaac. He was represented with various reptilian features and it was said that he dwelled in moist and wet places like caves. In his benevolent form, he was associated with giving life and creation, as the agriculture and all life depended on seasonal rains. Because of his importance, he was also important for the Maya kings who used his symbols to emphasize their authority. The god of lighting, K'awiil, was also important for the rulers' cult, and his symbols were engraved on the royal scepters. And, as maize was quintessential for the Maya survival, they also had a deity for that. In Popol Vuh he's known as Hun Hunahpu. He had two manifestations, as both an old and young maize god, and in essence, he was a benevolent god that represented abundance, prosperity and ultimately life. He's also notable as a god that died and was reborn, and as the father of the Hero Twins. Their names were Hunahpu and Xbanalque, and they played a crucial role in the creation of the present world.

In a shortened and simplified version of the creation myth, the gods created three worlds prior to the perfect and current version, which was among other things filled with humans made out of the maize dough. To make humans, first they needed to free maize to grow in the Middleworld, which was not possible as their father, the Maize God had been killed in the Underworld. The Hero Twins were invited to Xibalba to take part in series of tasks and a ball game created by the gods of death. One of the important tasks was sacrificing themselves and being revived, making self-sacrifice heroic act, which was important for the Maya rituals. In the end, they manage to beat the death gods and revive their father who then grows out of a turtle shell into the Middleworld. As he was reborn, maize was again available on the Kab, and from Kab the gods finally created humans. This fact is another religious explanation for sacrifices in the Maya world. If humans grow and eat maize, then it is normal that sustenance of gods would be humans, which they created. And as a reward for their feats, the Hero Twins ascend to the heaven.

Despite their triumph, at least one god of death prevailed. His name is Kimi, and he's usually shown either as a skeletal figure or as a bloated corpse. In addition to death, he's also related to war and all the consequences of war, including human sacrifice. Owls are also seen as the representation of death, as vicious night predators, and in some myths, they are even messengers of Kimi. Among many deities were two merchant gods, though two of them may be related, or be part of the same "deity complex". Both of them are shown carrying merchant packages, indicating trade and wealth. One of them known as Ek Chuaj is also a patron of cacao, an important trade resource and a form of currency. The other merchant god, whose name yet hasn't been decoded, is shown with a cigar in his mouth, depicting his connection to shamans, and he is considered to be one of the oldest gods. Interestingly both of them, besides wealth and trade, show signs of war and danger. The older merchant god is shown with attributes of an owl and a jaguar, both related to war and death. On the other hand, Ek Chuaj's connection is clearer, as he's shown carrying a spear. Through these symbols, the Maya represented the dangers that followed a life of merchants, who often had to defend themselves.

Fulfilling the role that, unlike the merchant gods, was more of cosmological importance was a god named Pawahtun. He was one of the gods that had quadripartite form, and each of his manifestations was tasked with holding one of the corners of the world. But despite his serious task as a world-bearer, he was often pictured drunk and in the company of young women. Even more important was a pair of so-called Paddler gods, which are depicted as rowers in a canoe. As they sit in the opposite sides of the canoe, they represent day and night, as they travel across the sky. Modern researchers named them Old Jaguar Paddler and Old Stingray Paddler, as they are represented by those animals. They are sometimes depicted traveling across the Underworld waters, which may indicate they had some connection with the transportation of the deceased to the afterlife. It was also suggested that the Paddler gods also played a role in the creation of the universe, but more common was their connection with ritual bloodletting and sacrifice. They are depicted in scenes of those rituals, while one of the more constant parts of the Paddler gods' imagery were some of the tools used in bloodletting ceremonies.

Not all Maya deities were male. An important role in their pantheon was played by two Moon goddesses, one young and one old, again representing duality in the Maya beliefs. The younger goddess, sometimes represented by a crescent moon and a rabbit, had her powers and godly duties overlapping with the Maize god, in form of fertility and abundance. This is probably connected to the lunar cycle, which was important for determining when to plant crops. That is why some scholars linked her, or at least one of her manifestations, with the Hun Hunahpu's wife. Other think she was paired with the Sun god, as the portrait of a ruler's mother was sometimes depicted within her symbol, while the solar sign was used for the father. Older Moon goddess, Ix Chel, served also as a rainbow deity, which was seen as the mark of the demons, leading to the Underworld. Due to that fact, she had a certain duality of good and evil within her. When connected with rainbow she was connected to storms, floods, disease, and ultimately destruction of the world. But when she was linked with the moon, she was associated with water as a source of life. She was then linked with creation, being the patron deity of medicine and childbirth, as well as divination and weaving. As such, she was married to Itzamná.

The Maya goddess Ix Chel. Source: https://commons.wikimedia.org

There is another important deity, which has to be mentioned to emphasize the fact that religion, as all other aspects of the Maya culture, was also influenced by contacts with other Mesoamerican civilizations. It is K'uk'ulcan, or as the Aztecs would call him, Quetzalcoatl. This deity, a famous Feathered Serpent of Mesoamerican religions, existed since the early days of the Maya. And, it may have been originally the product of Olmec influence. In those early days, K'uk'ulcan was more connected with war and conquest. But with the later contact with central Mexico, he became more connected with learning and merchants, while he was also a patron deity of rulers. He also served as a god of wind. K'uk'ulcan came to prominence only in the terminal Classic and Postclassic periods, becoming one of the central deities in Chichén Itzá and Mayapan. It is today considered that this shared reverence of the Feathered Serpent among all Mesoamericans helped to facilitate trade among people of different ethnic and social origins. But despite the origins of the people, Maya believed every living human possessed several souls. This is yet another example of the plurality in the Maya religion, to which exact details of number and nature are blurry.

It was believed that souls are eternal and that morality resided in them. It was considered that loss of a certain amount of souls led to sickness, and the shamans were tasked to cure patients by returning the souls to normal. Souls played an important part of shamanism in other forms. For example, it was believed that some of the souls were actually linked to the animal companion spirits, which was crucial for shamans and their connection to nature. Death arrived only when all souls had left the body. Some of the souls died along with the body, others traveled to the afterlife. It was also considered possible for certain types of souls to be reborn in a new person, possibly a future descendant, creating yet another link with of the Maya and their ancestors. With complicated and numerous souls, it is rather difficult to exactly specify in what kind of afterlife the Maya believed. There are certain ideas of an afterlife, with possible rewards and punishments similar to Christian heaven and hell. At the same time, the idea of reincarnation also existed. For kings, deification was also a possibility. The concept of an afterlife may have varied across different regions of the Maya world, as well as all other parts of the Maya religion, which is one reason why researchers find it difficult to puzzle out the complete picture about it. The truth is that both through time and across space, the Maya beliefs changed and had their own unique features, with certain central themes remaining the same. Yet there is no denying it was another part of the Maya civilization which showcased how elaborate and developed the Maya were.

Chapter 11 – The Maya everyday life

It is common in all civilizations of the world that artists and writers often focus their attention on the higher classes: their lives, rituals, and obligations. And historians, due to the more substantial evidence, also tend to give more time and effort in learning about them. It is pretty much the same with the Maya, and so far in this book, the main focus has been on the upper castes of the society. Yet the commoners constituted about 90% of the Maya population, and as such are at least equally important in the story of the Maya civilization. This chapter will be focused as much as possible on their lives, with only occasional throwbacks to the elite, mostly by way of comparison. One of the first important questions regarding the commoners was what their trades were. Today, estimates state that about 75% of the Maya population were involved in some type of food production. Men were mostly tasked with farming and hunting, while the women maintained kitchen gardens, foraged, and prepared food. It is likely that in some cases women helped their husbands in the field. Yet the food was produced year-round, and during the breaks, the Maya weaved, worked on constructions, made tools, or even served as warriors. The other 25%, including the elites, were professionals in different crafts. They were potters, artists, painters, sculptors, merchants, soldiers, priests, stonecutters, jewelers, artisan toolmakers, government officials, and others. Almost half of these non-farmers were members of the noble classes, and they held more socially-desired jobs of priests, soldiers, and even artists and jewelers.

One of the things that was common to all the classes was the importance of families. This was notably demonstrated by nobility, yet the commoners also paid a lot of attention to lineage. Most marriages seem to have been arranged by a third party, and it was forbidden to marry someone who had the same surname, to prevent mixing within the same family. Yet it was socially desirable that both newlyweds were from the same town and class. After the marriage, the husband and wife kept surnames of both their mother and father, to keep track of their lineage. In the first couple of years, the couple lived with the wife's family, where the husband worked to "pay off" the price for her hand. Then they moved to the husband's family where they built their own house and home. It should be noted that most of the Maya were monogamous, especially the commoners, and divorce was possible and seemingly easy to perform. Married couples started having children as soon as possible, with women praying to Ix Chel for fertility and easy childbirth. Babies, when born, were nursed as long as possible, even up to the age of five in some cases. It is at that age that they went through a ceremony in which they were clothed for the first time and became a more functional part of the family. As they grew older, passing through puberty, they would go through a public ritual signifying they became adults. After that, they usually waited for a marriage to be arranged for them. During this waiting period, it was expected of young women to behave chastely and modestly. On the other hand, men were freer, and some evidence points out they may have enjoyed the company of prostitutes. After they were married, both partners were expected to remain faithful.

Formal education didn't exist, and the family was supposed to teach its own children. Parents were in charge of teaching them traditional household tasks, farming techniques, and basics of tradition and religion. In cases of more specialized skills and trades, like pottery making or stonecutting, they learned and apprenticed with extended family members. In cases of the elites, there was some sort of formal education and training for trades that required more esoteric knowledge of rituals, astronomy, medicine, and of course literacy. A sort of school may have existed for scribes, though this may also have been more of an apprenticeship. Parents were also tasked with morally upbringing their offspring to become functional parts of the Maya society. This was important, as the punishment for crimes could be severe. Perpetrators of violent crimes as murder, arson, and rape were usually sentenced to death by sacrifice, stoning, or even dismembering. Though in case of murder, the victim's family may ask for material retribution instead. This was a norm for property crime like theft, where the offender either paid back what he took or was enslaved until he worked off his debt. Adultery was also a serious crime, but mostly for men, who often suffered death penalties, while it was considered that public humiliation was sufficient for women. And this inequality under the law was common in social status as well. A thief of noble descent had his entire face tattooed as a symbol of his disgrace, while the killing of a slave wasn't seen as a serious offense. It is also likely that some laws prohibited commoners to adorn themselves with items connected with nobility, like exotic feathers, pelts, and jewelry. High-ranking town officials, often from noble descent, acted as judges, and though it would be likely they would be partial in some cases, most sources tell us that they acted impartially.

And as the family was the core of the Maya society, their households played an important part in their everyday life. Those were usually composed of several buildings, used for both accommodation and storage, centered around a patio or a courtyard. And it was common for several generations to live in the same household. This pattern was followed no matter the class or wealth of the family, going from the simple clay and thatch cottages of the commoners to the stone palaces of the royal family. The buildings also served as work areas for making homemade pottery, tools, baskets, clothing, and cooking. The food of the commoners varied, but on most days, they ate simple dishes made from squash, beans, and of course maize. Those were complimented with herbs, other vegetables, fruit, and meat. They also made various drinks, most notably a warm maize gruel called atole, and a fermented drink chicha. Nobles also drank a chocolate drink for which it seems a Central Mexican name, xocoatl was used. It is also interesting that famous Mexican tortillas weren't that common among the Maya. According to the remains found, even Maya commoners were well fed and healthy.

Besides good nutrition, an important part of maintaining health was cleanliness. The Maya cleaned their homes, washed their hands and mouth after eating, and occasionally took steam baths. These baths may have been part of certain religious rituals. The Maya shamans also performed curing rituals, likely connected to the idea of the missing souls previously explained. But those were also paired with various herbal cures and ointments. And though some were rather efficient and potent, even relieving some heart conditions, other were completely counterproductive. For example, the Maya believed that smoking tobacco would cure asthma. Besides health and hygiene, they also cared a lot about their looks. And while for us today their ideas of beauty seem unimaginable, they put a lot of effort into it. Most notable was the ideal of elongated and back-sloped foreheads. This was achieved by flattening the still-soft foreheads of babies with two pieces of wood tightly bound on the back and the front of the head. In earlier research, it was assumed this was done only by nobles, as a sign of their stature. But recent surveys show it was actually done by most of the Maya, probably in the attempt to resemble the maize cob.

Another, by today's standards, strange ideal of beauty in the Maya society were slightly crossed eyes. This was also achieved at a very young age, by tying tiny strand balls in front of the baby's eyes, making them focus on it. More relatable to modern fashion were practices of tattoos and piercings. Tattoos were done in a very painful way, by scarring the painted skin, infusing the pigment in the scars. Because of that, as well as the fact it could easily cause infections, tattoos weren't that common and were mostly done to prove and showcase personal bravery. On the other hand, piercings were more common, with ear, lip and nose plugs, which were often adorned by wealthy nobles with precious stones and colorful shells. Both of these practices were done by men and women, though in slightly different fashion and measure. Interestingly, men had not only more tattoos but also more piercings, which was also used to indicate someone's position in the society. A tradition which didn't leave permanent marks was body painting. Warriors used red and black paint to look fiercer and more dangerous. Priests were sometimes painted in blue, for their religious rituals, while women used various colors to emphasize their beauty, almost like makeup. Black paint was also used by people involved in cleansing and other rituals, as well as for ceremonial fasting.

The hairstyle was also an important factor in the Maya style and beauty. It seems that both men and women wore long hair. Male hairstyles were simpler; sides were cut short, while the back was kept long. They usually kept it in ponytails, but sometimes the long tresses were braided with feathers or ribbons. Women had their long hair arranged into elegant and adorned braids and headdresses, more commonly adorned with feathers, ribbons, and other types of accessories. It is also possible that the front of their heads was shaved, to emphasize their elongated foreheads, but this may only be an artistic representation that heightened the desired look. In reality, it is rather difficult to pinpoint the exact look of Maya hairstyles as they are often depicted wearing elaborate headdresses and hats used in various rituals and ceremonies. Men usually avoided beards, and though some of the rulers were depicted with them this was possibly fake, and something worn only for ceremonial purposes. And, as the Maya lived in hot and tropical climates, they used perfume and ointments to lessen their body odors. There were made with various herbs and fruits, though it seems vanilla perfume was the most common.

A figurine of a Maya female. Source: https://commons.wikimedia.org

And although most of the ideals of beauty and fashion were rather similar for both sexes, clothing was somewhat different. Women wore skirts, blouses, and used scarf-like jackets and sarongs around their torsos. Not all women covered their breasts. Beneath their skirts women wore breechcloths. Men wore long capes and only breechcloths, though sometimes they are depicted wearing something looking like a male skirt or a kilt. Complicated robes and jackets were worn mostly by nobles performing rituals. The more formal clothing was often adorned with embroidered feathers, pelts, and symbols of the gods. Regular clothing, especially items worn by the commoners, were less ornate, yet possibly brightly colored. To emphasize their looks, the Maya also had non-piercing jewelry like necklaces, collars, pendants, belts, and bracelets. Again, men wore them more than women, as they were an important indicator of the social status. The material used to make those varied both through time and between the classes. While nobles used various precious stones, most notably jade, as well as precious shells, and later gold, commoners used more often wood and bone, sometimes colored to make it more special.

But good looks and trinkets weren't the only vital part of the Maya everyday life, nor did they provide fun and excitement. For that, they had various entertainment. Most important were, of course, great religious ceremonies, that lasted for days, with music, dancing, and feasts. But these weren't meant for everyday amusement. For that they played a variety of board games, they gambled, and played less brutal types of ball games, played on simple dirt fields, without any religious meaning behind them. They also sang and danced, again without many ritual connotations, and some researchers believe that certain types of codices were written for public readings and performances, resembling a theatrical show. Nobles also had banquets and private feasts, with a lot of food, drinking, and various entertainment like musicians and jesters. Also, an important part of the Maya society were more private family celebrations for events like weddings and ancestor anniversaries, which also provided some leisure time. But all this entertainment was probably less common than we would consider normal today since most of the Maya, especially the commoners, had to work hard throughout the day, and didn't have too much leisure time. But despite that it seems that in most cases, everyday life of the Maya wasn't all that bad, leaving most of them healthy, happy, and well fed.

Chapter 12 – From colonial times to today, the Maya persist

Many books about Maya history and civilization end with the arrival of the Spanish conquistadors. After a brief description of how they were overpowered by technologically superior Europeans, aided by diseases, the Maya story ends. It almost looks like a conscious decision made by the historians to alienate the present-day Maya from the greatness of their ancestors and their culture. And it also sends a message to the world that Maya civilization died under the colonial rule. Though it is true that it was severely altered and influenced by the Spaniards, mostly in religious matters, it would be wrong to think all of their traditions were abandoned, in spite of the Spanish colonial government doing all it could to make the Maya forget about their past. With about 90% of the Maya population ravaged by diseases, the colonial government was instructed to gather up what remained of the Maya and concentrate them in villages and towns built to resemble Spanish settlements in Europe. There it would be easier for them to control and convert the indigenous population. And though some of the Maya resisted until the end of 17th century, eventually pretty much all of them were relegated to the settlements.

In centers of all new settlements were two main buildings, a church and a seat of the civil government. With furious zeal the new masters worked on converting the Maya, pressuring them to forget their gods, mythology, ceremonies, and rituals, to burn their books and erase their traditional writing system. Instead, they offered them their one god, the savior Jesus, The Bible, and the Latin alphabet. Ritual human sacrifices further fueled the religious fervor of Christian priests in converting newly conquered population. They deemed it as satanic, evil, and completely immoral. Yet they found that the burning of infidels at the stakes, torturing them in various cruel manners, and all other practices associated with the Spanish Inquisition, were completely fine, moral, and in accordance with "civilized" nations. At the same time, colonial masters also imposed new civil and government systems. For one, the Maya lost their independence and their voice, while at the same time being used almost as a slave workforce and forced to pay taxes and tributes. Spaniards also changed the economy of the region, introducing steel tools, domestic animals, and ultimately shutting down local trade as every valuable resource from the Maya homeland was shipped to Europe.

But despite all the degradation of everything Maya under the Spanish rule, the Maya culture and civilization managed to survive. Though their religion was ultimately lost, certain aspects managed to fuse with Christianity and survive. One of those was respect for their ancestors, while in some cases Christian rituals were updated with local practices. In some cases, even the sacrifices continued, though they were performed on animals, mostly chickens. And some of the more educated Maya used the newly adopted Latin alphabet to transcribe at least some of their traditional books, like Popol Vuh, saving certain elements of their culture in them. Among other aspects of the culture they preserved were symbols and patterns they used on their clothes, though these were also mixed with Christian symbolism and done on European-styled clothing. But most importantly the Maya preserved their own Mayan language. But thanks to the separation of different groups of the Maya, their language, as well as other traditions, grew apart during the colonial rule. With that the colonial and postcolonial Maya population and their civilization, was fractured and separated, again lacking the unity to fight for its own needs.

But it should be noted that the conquest of the Maya heartland wasn't completely successful. Despite trying to "civilize" the Maya, the Spanish lords and the Ladinos, non-elite Spaniards and Hispanicized people, lived separately from them. And as they were outnumbered, they lived in confined communities. Around and in between them was the local Maya population, which was more than aware of the differences between them. Essentially, attempts of the colonial government to assimilate and incorporate the local population into their own civilization were thwarted by their own disdain towards the Maya. They were treated as lower-class citizens, basically without any rights. And for a very long time, the Maya had to put up with that because they had no power to fight back. But in the 19th century, the Spanish Colonial Empire crumbled and new Mesoamerican states sprouted up. In spite of certain expectations that with the colonial system gone the locals, including the Maya, would live better, basically nothing changed. Descendants of Ladinos continued to rule the countries, oppressing the Maya the same as before. And finally, that led the Maya to rebel.

The Yucatec Maya took up guns and in 1847 started the war against the Mexican central government. For the white elite that exploited them, this became known as the "War of the Castes," which is yet another confirmation that they saw the Maya as the lowest class of people. During this rebellion, it seems that ancient warrior spirits woke up among the Maya fighters as they managed to take over control of almost all of Yucatan. Mexican government troops were confined into a few cities on the coast. For a short period of time, it seemed like the conquest was reversed and that they gained back their freedom. But as the planting season came, the Maya army just like in the pre-Columbian times returned to their homes to work on their fields. However, this wasn't the end of this uprising. The skirmishes and localized fighting continued, but in 1850 a new upsurge in fighting spirit happened within the Maya. They were inspired by the manifestation of so-called "Talking Cross," through which they thought God communicated to them, telling them to continue their struggle. Once again, religion was infused with warfare, and with newfound power, the Maya of the southeast Yucatan managed to fight off the government troops and establish their semi-independent state. It is often called Chan Santa Cruz, named by its capital just like in the heyday of the Maya civilization.

The question of independence of this Maya state is rather complicated. The Mexican central government didn't have any control over that territory, the Maya were factually free. But except Britain, no other country recognized its separation from Mexico City. And the only reason why Britain did so was because of the trade between British Belize and Chan Santa Cruz. There are also some suggestions that some of the weapons used in the rebellion came from Belize. Other smaller groups of the Maya also declared their own independent path, but they were less successful. Some of those groups even opposed the Chan Santa Cruz as they saw worshiping of the Talking Cross as swerving from the path of true Christianity. And of course, the central Mexican government didn't remain passive , it attacked the Chan Santa Cruz, even arriving close to the capital on a few occasions. Fighting continued for the next 50 years, with the major turning point happening in 1893 when Britain signed a treaty with Mexico, in which among other things it was recognized that Chan Santa Cruz was under Mexican sovereignty. This was a major setback for the Maya because they couldn't resupply their weapons and ammunition from Belize. And in 1901 they were finally defeated by the government troops. It is estimated that during this war between 40 and 50 thousand people died, mostly Maya.

Oil painting of Caste War, c1850. Source: https://commons.wikimedia.org

Despite losing the war and their freedom, there were some positive consequences of this Maya uprising. Around 1915, the central government implemented certain reforms. Among these were agrarian reforms that abolished colonial labor system, and that solved some of the problems that caused the revolt. But, of course, the Maya were still treated as second-class citizens, and their position, in general, didn't improve much. And as the Maya themselves didn't care much about integration into the Mexican society, they remained relatively separated both politically and economically, living mostly as poor farmers. But the policy of Mexico City changed in the 1950s and 60s. Through many initiatives they tried to modernize and incorporate the Maya into the Mexican community, creating a migration of the Maya by offering them unused lands, as well as parts of the jungle they could clear, so they could create new farms. These initiatives were of very limited success, and the biggest consequence was rising anger of the non-indigenous Mexicans who felt their land was given to the Maya. That is why by the 1970s these initiatives were stopped. But at approximately the same time, the Maya of Guatemala went through the darkest period since the arrival of the Spanish conquistadors.

During that period Central American countries were sucked into the whirlwind of the Cold War, where the leftist rebels, backed by some socialist countries and some of the indigenous population hoping for more equal society, clashed with the right-wing military dictatorship supported by the United States. As part of this wider political problem the Civil War in Guatemala started in 1960, and from the beginning one of the major targets of the right-winged government were the Maya. Though their limited support to the rebels played a part in this decision, more often it was caused because of racism and intolerance of the Ladino government towards the Maya, whom they often saw as impure and unworthy. Ultimately for them, the Maya were the hated lower race. The terror towards the indigenous population escalated from 1975 to 1985, during which period the Guatemalan army carried out more than 600 massacres and destroyed more than 400 Maya villages. Somewhere between 150 and 200 thousand people were killed, more than 40 thousand "disappeared," and around 100 thousand women were raped. Besides those, there were about half a million refugees that sought security in surrounding countries and in the US. The vast majority of these victims were the Maya, with estimates varying from 80 to 90%. Some other smaller indigenous groups were targeted as well. The Civil War lasted until the mid-1990's, but its consequences are still felt today.

After the civil war ended, this terror was internationally recognized as a genocide, usually called the Guatemalan genocide or the Maya genocide. Another, though a less used name was Silent Holocaust, partially because it seemed that no one cared about the Maya victims as the genocide occurred. They were silenced and ignored by the majority of the world who was much more interested in the Cold War aspect of the Civil War. A United Nations commission even concluded that part of the responsibility for the massacres should be laid on America's training of the Guatemalan officers in the counterinsurgency techniques, though this brought no consequences for the United States. And, as the Guatemalan Maya finally found some peace in the 90's, things once again turned for worse for the Mexican Maya. The main issue was that, in order to join the North American Free Trade Agreement (NAFTA) with the US and Canada, Mexico had to modify certain articles in its constitution, among others one that protected the communal indigenous land. That land was the main source of food and income for many Maya, as well as some other native groups. With redaction of that article, the central government could privatize and sell those lands. Furthermore, the local population that depended on those communal farms became illegal land-squatters, and their communities became informal settlements.

Once again, the central government was deaf to the Maya complaints and it amended the Mexican constitution. This caused an armed revolt of the Maya in January of 1994, which this time occurred in the Mexican state of Chiapas instead of Yucatan. The Zapatista Army of National Liberation led the insurgency, with demands for cultural, political, social, and land rights for all the Maya in Mexico, as well as for all other indigenous population in the country. The Mexican army quickly responded and after only 12 days the ceasefire was announced. Yet this event shocked the Mexican government. Politicians in Mexico City weren't used to the idea of indigenous people revolting so openly. But more worrying for them was the support the movement gained across Mexico and across the world. The Maya achieved that through excellent use of media, especially the internet, which was still a new technology at the time. Under pressure, the government agreed to negotiate with the Maya and promised that the native population of Mexico would be protected. Yet as soon as the dust settled they continued with their own plans, the same way as before. And to this day the Maya protest, trying to get their voices heard, while the Mexican politicians are more and more trying to avoid them, ignoring them. In those tense situations, some local fight and skirmishes do occur, but mostly between civil populations, and there are no signs of improvement.

Today Maya of all countries live in relative peace, although their lives are far from ideal. Rainforests are being destroyed, their traditional farms are taken from them, substituted with cattle ranches; the army is a looming threat. Yet they are still fighting for their political rights, and in recent years the Maya leaders are slowly realizing the only possible solution for their salvation is connecting all the various Maya groups living in all Mesoamerican states. Despite their linguistic differences, working together is the only way to preserve their culture, tradition, and history. Yet the last couple of decades another change has occurred. With extra attention, both from science circles and from media made their civilization better known to the world. With interesting culture, breathtaking remains and colorful nature around them the Maya became rather popular in tourist circles. More and more visitors arrive in their communities, owing to the greatness of the Maya past. And this is a double-edged sword. On one side, no country would dare to commit atrocities as before, both because of the negative media image but also because of the economic impact of tourism. Of course, economic gains are also beneficial to the Maya, who are now able to earn more money and are less dependent on farming. Also, their culture is now much harder to destroy, as it has become more recognizable and popular.

A Maya woman making souvenirs. Source: https://commons.wikimedia.org

And that is where the blade strikes back on the Maya. Most tourists come to the Maya with certain expectation what they should and want to see. And in those expectations are many common misconceptions and half-truths, to which some of the Maya pander. They don't want to lose the customers that bring in much-needed income. And under that pressure, tourists at the same time save and change the Maya culture. Also, in a way, tourism degrades their rich culture and traditions into something trivial. Their craftwork and art are reduced to a trifle bought in the flea market as a keepsake from the trip. For them, there is no deeper meaning to it. But for now, there is no alternative for most of the Maya people. And considering both political situations and tourism begs the question of the Maya future. While there is great danger lurking for them, there is no doubt they will prevail. As so many times in the past, they will adapt and overcome obstacles, trying to maintain their traditions and civilization.

Conclusion

Hopefully, through this guide, you have gained the basic understanding of who the Maya are, what their culture and civilization represent. You now see how complex and intricate their history was, with their political struggles, alliances, and wars between their ancient states and developed societies. And, you have learned how crucial their role was in the Mesoamerican region, connecting it through trade, sharing ideas, culture, and mythology with civilizations around them. More importantly, it should be obvious that the Maya weren't some backward savages that lived in the jungles before the Europeans came to show them what true civilization means. They created stunning art, grand architectural marvels comparable with the ancient wonders of the world and tracked the stars and planets with unbelievable precision. And although their view of the world was rather different from how we perceive it today, it was no less elaborate and well-thought through. Their religion, despite the controversial sacrifices, was a complicated system of beliefs, myths, moral guidelines, and rituals. And in no way should it be considered primitive or less worthy than any other ancient religions. Also, seeing some aspects of their everyday life should bring them closer to us, with the understanding that they too lived their lives filled with hopes and fears, worries and celebrations. This makes them feel less like relics of the past and more like humans that are still around.

Ultimately this guide should have explained why the Maya civilization should be respected and equally praised, along with many other ancient civilizations. At the same time, it stands as a reminder that the Maya, unlike most other praised civilizations of the past, never disappeared. Not only are they still around, but they are trying to preserve their heritage and traditions, fighting for survival. And that fact should be a constant reminder that history isn't always something that happened long ago in a distant land, but something that is still present, echoing in the world of today. The story of the Maya struggle in the recent times should also stand as inspiration that no matter how dark things look, as long as there are people willing to fight, there is still hope. Because of that, respect of the Maya civilization should be extended to the people keeping it alive today, the Maya people of our times. Understanding all that should, in the end, show why it is important for world cultural heritage that the story of the Maya isn't forgotten, and why it should be kept for future generations as well.

Of course, this is a task that goes beyond what this single book can do. So, in the end, this guide, educational and informative, as well as fun and interesting, was supposed to serve only as an introduction to the Maya world, both past, and present. It builds a solid foundation upon which further knowledge should be built. And hopefully, it will light a spark of interest, amazement, and intrigue about the Maya civilization, as there is so much more about it to be told. It is exactly through that spark, that thirst for more knowledge and a deeper understanding of the Maya that this book serves the higher goal. Through that, we make our own contribution, no matter how small, to the preservation of the beautiful, intriguing, and unique Maya civilization.

Check out more Captivating History books

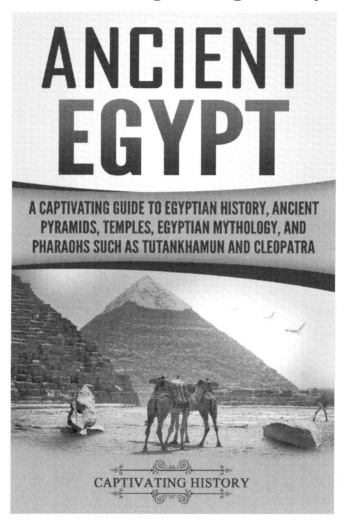

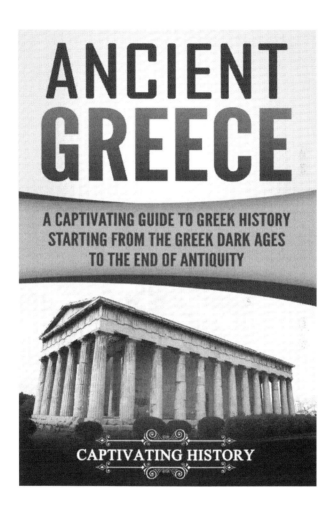

ANCIENT GREECE

A CAPTIVATING GUIDE TO GREEK HISTORY STARTING FROM THE GREEK DARK AGES TO THE END OF ANTIQUITY

CAPTIVATING HISTORY

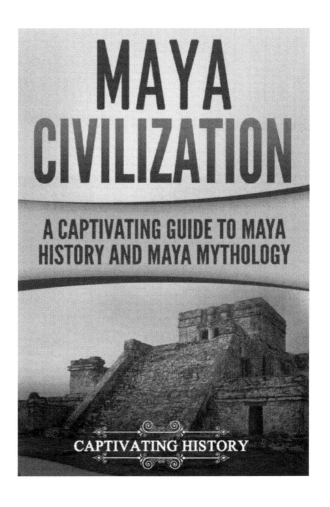

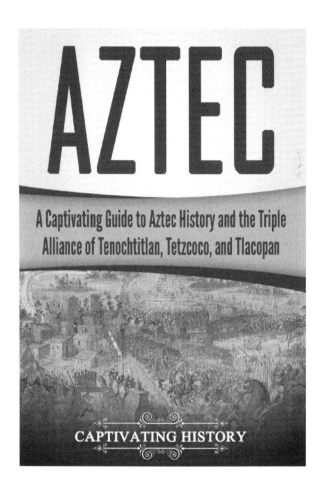

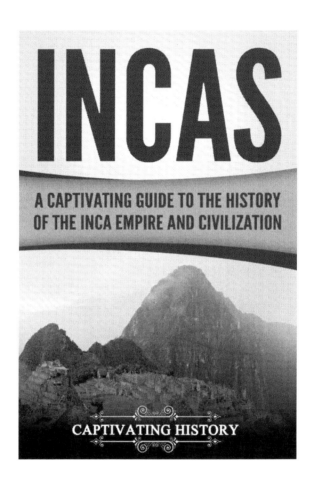

Bibliography:

Adams Richard E. W. and MacLeod Murdo J., *The Cambridge history of the native peoples of the Americas Volume II: Mesoamerica, part 1*, Cambridge, Cambridge University Press, 2008.

Adams Richard E. W. and MacLeod Murdo J., *The Cambridge history of the native peoples of the Americas Volume II: Mesoamerica, part 2*, Cambridge, Cambridge University Press, 2008.

Ardren Traci, *Ancient Maya wome*n, Lanham, Rowman & Littlefield Publishers, Inc., 2002.

Carmack R.M., Gasco J. and Gossen G.H., *The Legacy of Mesoamerica: History and Culture of a Native American Civilization*, New York, Routledge, 2007.

Coe Michael D., *Breaking the Maya code*, London, Thames and Hudson, 2012.

Coe Michael D. and Houston Stephen, *The Maya: 9th edition*, London, Thames and Hudson, 2015.

Foias Antonia E., *Ancient Maya Political Dynamics*, Tampa, University Press of Florida, 2013.

Foster Lynn V., *Handbook to life in the Ancient Maya world*, New York, Facts On File, Inc., 2002.

George Charles and Linda, *Maya civilization*, Farmington Hills, Lucent Books, 2010.

Goetz Delia, *Popol Vuh: The sacred book of Ancient Quiche Maya*, Norman, University of Oklahoma Press, 1950.

Hassig Ross, *War and Society in Ancient Mesoamerica*, Berkley, University of California press, 1992.

Koontz R., Reese-Taylor K. and Headrick A., *Landscape and power in ancient Mesoamerica*, Boulder, Westview Press, 2001.

Kurnick Sarah and Baron Joanne, *Political strategies in pre-Columbian Mesoamerica*, Boulder, University Press of Colorado, 2016.

Lohse Jon C. and Valdez Jr. Fred, *Ancient Maya commoners*, Austin, University of Texas Press, 2004.

Mazariegos Oswaldo C., *Art and Myth of the Ancient Maya*, London, Yale University Press, 2017.

McKillop Heather I., *The ancient Maya: new perspectives*, Santa Barbara, ABC-CLIO, Inc., 2004.

Sharer Robert J., *Daily life in Maya civilization*, London, Greenwood Press, 2009.

Thompson John S.E., *Maya history and religion*, Norman, University of Oklahoma Press, 1990.

Werness-Rude Maline D. and Spencer Kaylee R., *Maya imagery, architecture, and activity: space and spatial analysis in art history*, Albuquerque, University of New Mexico Press, 2015.

Free Bonus from Captivating History (Available for a Limited time)

Hi History Lovers!

Now you have a chance to join our exclusive history list so you can get your first history ebook for free as well as discounts and a potential to get more history books for free! Simply visit the link below to join.

Captivatinghistory.com/ebook

Also, make sure to follow us on:

Twitter: @Captivhistory

Facebook: Captivating History:@captivatinghistory